BEST *of* AUSTRALIAN POEMS

2022

First published 2022 by
Australian Poetry
www.australianpoetry.com

This book is copyright. Aside from fair dealing for the purposes of study, research, criticism, review, or as otherwise permitted under the Copyright Act, no part may be reproduced by any process without written permission. Inquiries should be addressed to the publisher. Individual poem's copyright retained by the authors.

National Library of Australia
Cataloguing-in-Publication data:

Best of australian poems 2022
ISBN: 978-0-9923189-3-2

Series Publisher: Australian Poetry
BoAP 2022 AP Editorial: Jacinta Le Plastrier (Publisher),
Adalya Nash Hussein & Jennifer Nguyen (Editorial Associates)
Cover and Design: Sophie Gaur
Printed by Lightning Source International

Publisher Note:
AP would like to deeply thank all the publishers, platforms, and other organisations that support the flourishing and publishing of Australian poetry. While some of these *BoAP 2022* poems were selected in open call-out, many were previously published by these great forces. It is AP's policy as Publisher to also keep 'arm's length' completely in the selection of poems by our guest editors, where we have different guest editors across our numerous, annual publications. Regarding *BoAP 2022*, we do work to ensure that poems fall within the set, strict timeframe. AP's house style is to accept a poet's choice of titling capitalisation, choice of punctuation, and spelling styles, so across the book there is a natural variation allowed. Finally a number of patrons have contributed funds to this particular project. To these, and our core funders and project partners, profound thanks.
This project has been assisted by the Australian Government through the Australia Council, its arts funding and advisory body.

BEST *of* AUSTRALIAN POEMS

2022

GUEST EDITORS
JEANINE LEANE
&
JUDITH BEVERIDGE

ACKNOWLEDGEMENT
OF COUNTRY

Australian Poetry is based
in Naarm, Melbourne, working
in offices and remotely on both
Wurundjeri Woi Wurrung and
Boon Wurrung lands.
We acknowledge their Elders, past,
present and emerging. As a national
poetry body, we also acknowledge
that we work across many lands, and
communities, and we extend our
deep respect to all First Peoples, not
just in Australia, but across the globe,
including poets and audiences, and
their enduring connection
to Country.

Best of Australian Poems
SERIES PUBLISHER
Australian Poetry

Foreword

We acknowledge that the collation, production, reading for and editing of *Best of Australian Poems 2022* took place on the traditional lands of the Ngunnawal, Ngambri, Wallumedegal, Dhurag, Wiradjuri and Boon Wurrung and Wurundjeri Woi Wurrung First Nations peoples. These lands were never ceded. Always was and always will be Aboriginal land.

During 2021-22 Australia lost several poets: Jordie Albiston (1961-2022), John Carey (1942-2022), Evan Jones (1931-2022), Craig Powell (1940-2022) and Nicolette Stasko (1950-2021). We acknowledge their contribution to Australian poetry and mourn their passing and encourage you to seek out and engage with their numerous works. We have chosen to open *Best of Australian Poems 2022* with the final two stanzas from 'Press On' by Jordie Albiston:

> Yes, guide your hands to your father's piano, and give them
> up gently to familiar chords: raise your eyes to the long light
> ahead, and press on. Though the heart has atrophied and the
>
> numberless moments you thought you possessed have gone:
> through the catacombs of conscience, the dreamless dawn
> and the unfinished night filled with silent guests, press on.

Best of Australian Poems 2022 is the second annual anthology from the national poetry organisation Australian Poetry (AP) in what is hoped to be an ongoing series. AP initiated the series in 2021 in response to both poets' and readers' appetites for a new annual poetic snapshot after the prestigious, long running *The Best Australian Poems* series produced by Black Inc. concluded some years ago.

Following on from last year's highly-regarded diverse collection of poetry, guest-edited by Ellen van Neerven and Toby Fitch, *Best of Australian Poems 2022* strives to bring together 100 of Australia's most poignant, original, and challenging works by poets over slightly more than a year's timeframe (1 July 2021 – 7 August 2022). Ellen and Toby set a high bar with the extent of their reading and sourcing of poems. In our 2022 selections we also hope to reflect the year that has been in a cartography of poetry that speaks to some of the hopes, concerns, fears, critiques, and aspirations across the many different diasporas of peoples who have settled here since 1788 and made Australia their home alongside the Nation's First Peoples.

Given that the anthology contains only 100 poems out of the many thousands we read, it is obvious that many excellent pieces missed out on inclusion. Different editors make different choices, and many excellent volumes could have been compiled from the available poems. When collating a national anthology, many factors come in to play, especially in trying to represent the different states and territories as well as gender, identity, and ethnic diversity. The variety and vitality of the poems preserved in this anthology are representative of the rich, imaginative approaches Australian poets are currently employing. Our aim was to be inclusive and respectful of differing and divergent poetics, and while poets may not always agree on what makes a poem memorable or exceptional, this anthology demonstrates that our poetry is as strong and powerful as any other art form in the country. We hope this book will bring new audiences and attention to poetry.

In an anthology bearing the weighty title of *Best of Australian Poems*, it is both a timely and fitting space for contemporary poets to consider all that the nation and continent of Australia is—and isn't—as some poets deftly and passionately articulate. Poetic responses are as varied as the demographic of the nation itself. The many phases and facets of what constitutes Australia, and what different meanings and perspectives this land holds for those who live and write here is a central concern of this anthology.

Around four thousand poems were formally submitted for this year's volume—over a third of the poems in this anthology come from those submissions. In addition to this, we read dozens of individual collections, both full-length and chapbooks, along with selected collections. As editors we also read widely across Australian on-line and print journals, magazines, and newspapers. We looked across exhibitions that included poetry, listened to readings and seminars, and watched performance poetry. Over half the poems in this volume have been previously published within the timeframe, but there are also previously unpublished works written over the time. We also read the works of poets currently in detention on Australian soil in the hope of representing those incarcerated as a result of the racial politics that have dominated Australia's treatment of people since the invasion. Unfortunately, due to a process of permissions, we were not able to publish their works.

It was impossible for us to read every poem that was written and published in the given timeframe. It is important to acknowledge the limitations of the textual space to represent certain works, such as poetry that exists in purely oral form, spontaneous poetry of the streets, rallies, demonstrations, community theatres and community events and gatherings. We acknowledge the value of these works that thrive outside of the written/printed form, and the rich contribution spoken word, oral, performance and protest poems bring to Australian literary culture, and the need for these diverse and rigorous forms to be recognised through some other mediums and platforms.

Reading the poems was a monumental task, but it was also a labour of love. We held numerous zoom meetings, and we brought differing and coinciding reading and writing expertise to the process. Along the way, we learnt much from each other's processes and methods; we were able to remain open to each other's poetic preferences, and in addition to the privilege of immersing ourselves in some of Australia's best poetry for 2021-2022, we came away from the editorial process with a greatly enriched and more expansive understanding of Australian poetry.

In this volume you will find narrative poems, prose poems, lyric poems, ekphrastic poems, archival poems, documentary poems, found poems, poems sourced from performance, spoken word or slam poetry, protest poems, poems that expose the duplicity of the 'Australian Dream', poems that critique national narratives and selective histories, eco-poems, translations, and poems in other languages, including First Nations languages, concrete poems, conceptual poems, long poems, short poems, elegies, epistolary poems, surrealist poems, and more. There are poems which critique and challenge the current socio-economic status quo, poems that critique and challenge racism, colonialism, structural privilege, and systematic inequalities; poems that call for social justice; poems that grapple with climate change, global warming, and infinite consumption on a finite planet. Some poets contend with religion, spirituality, philosophy, mythology, and mythmaking; others are expressions of body, gender, non-binary experience, and states of being. Some poems focus on introspection—such as memory, locale, emotions, fragments, and episodes; others focus outwardly on the geo-political, on globalism and international movements. There are poems of flora and fauna; the relationships between humans and nature; poems that consider alternative realms and different planes of reality. And of course, given the environmental, political, and human turmoil of the last three years, there are poems that reflect on fires, floods, war, and the pandemic.

Poems within this collection challenge, expand and redefine the limits of what poetry is and can be and give new shape and form to Australia's evolving literary landscape. Through form, content, style and visual impact, these poems challenge the limits and confines of an existing literary canon to bring new voices, new themes, considerations, and concerns to the fore. In reading for and curating this volume, we considered poetry's capacity to crystallize, disrupt, refuse, expose, challenge, inform, or confirm the spectacle of Australian life.

We also believe there can be a power in bringing together, in a co-editing model, the editors' differing viewpoints. Poetry is not just about subject matter or content, it is also about a wide raft of craft and aesthetic values. Not everyone agrees what these values are. It is a contentious issue as to who decides what makes a good poem and one always needs to question received values and the cultural and political contexts in which art is made. Various lineages of poetic approaches work in different ways. Tools, such as repeating structures, like rhythm, assonance, alliteration, a recurrence of words, phrases, images, and formal constraints act as regulating mechanisms, not only for the breath, but also for the movement of thought. These specific and concentrated tools of poetry can enable a more intense and a more visceral connection with language than reading a report or a newspaper article. This is one form of connection that poetry has with the body and enables it its power as a 'felt' experience, as one in which body, mind and heart are involved. In other approaches to poetics, these tools might be rearranged or refused, even undermined in ways which are intended to destabilize and resist.

There are poems in this anthology from writers with a wide range of cultural backgrounds, ages, genders, and from all states and territories of Australia. There are also poems from Australian poets living or travelling overseas. Here, we aimed to bring as broad a cross-section of the socio-cultural fabric of the nation that is possible within the textual space of an anthology. Some of Australia's long-standing poets are featured here, alongside new, and emerging voices. In curating our chosen poems, we considered a range of options before deciding to stay with last year's model of presenting poems in alphabetical order by title. This centres the poem first, and allows for an organic cadence to develop and flow across the collection.

The page, however blank and benign it may seem, is never a neutral space. Under the pen of the poet each work reflects a slice of national consciousness, and in this way, poetry is a barometer of collective consciousness. We are conscious as we write this that despite significant pressure over many decades, Australia is the only settler colony that still has no treaty with the nation's First Peoples, and there is no voice to Parliament for Aboriginal and Torres Strait Islander peoples. We denounce both national and international injustices and atrocities that occurred as we edited, such as the senseless and horrific death of another Aboriginal teenager in Western Australia, Cassius Turvey, and the killing of Mahsa Amini, the young Iranian woman beaten in prison—resulting in her death—by the religious, morality police of Iran's government for not wearing a hijab in accordance with government standards.

We would like to thank every poet who submitted and who published works over our specific 2021 – 2022 timeframe. We are conscious that many poets could not be represented in this volume because they did not publish within the time frame, or did not submit work for consideration. We would also like to thank AP—especially Jacinta Le Plastrier, designer Sophie Gaur, Adalya Nash Hussein and Jennifer Nguyen—who have worked tirelessly over long hours to bring the artefact this volume is to the poetry reading public. We would also like to thank the Wheeler Centre for their partnership with AP and for hosting the launch of *Best of Australian Poems 2022*.

All poetry is story telling—an exchange between writer and reader—a meeting place, an invitation into another's experience, history, standpoint, insight, commentary. Collectively the poetry in this book tells an important part of Australia's story.

—*Jeanine Leane, Judith Beveridge*

Foreword		v
A Poem In Honour Of A Lioness Perfecting Her Balance Of Inner/Outer Power	SISTA ZAI ZANDA	1
Ableism is the pre-existing condition that puts us at risk	ANDY JACKSON	3
After Franz Marc, *The Dreamer* (1912)	PETER BOYLE	4
All Markets are All Universes	LIONEL FOGARTY	5
Anyhow Poem	LOUIS KLEE	6
Art for art's sake	THUY ON	8
Art That Moves	JESSICA L WILKINSON	9
Aubade, Allegro	ALEX SKOVRON	11
'Australianesque'	MICHAEL FARRELL	12
The Bees	CLAIRE POTTER	14
Being My Grandmothers (After Uluru)	JENNIFER KEMARRE MARTINIELLO OAM	15
Blame the Greenies	CATH DRAKE	17
book of hours	HARRY REID	18
Briefly on the Mountain	KRISTEN LANG	20
buried light	ALISON J BARTON	22
Buzz Words	ANN VICKERY	24
Canticle for a Dancing Man	STEPHEN GILFEDDER	25
Case # 70	SAMAH SABAWI	26
Choice Cuts	MYKAELA SAUNDERS	28
Cicadas	DIMITRA HARVEY	31
Closet Monster	SAMUEL WAGAN WATSON	34
Coast banksia	ANNE ELVEY	36
'COVID'	GAVIN YUAN GAO	37
Crowning	CAITLIN MALING	39
Death by Vertigo	DAKOTA FEIRER	45
The Earwig	AUDREY MOLLOY	47

Elephant Rocks | RENEÉ PETTITT-SCHIPP	50
Entanglement | TOBY FITCH	51
Extracts | SUZI MEZEI	53
Family mathematics | TRICIA DEARBORN	54
The Far East | ADAM AITKEN	58
First Reading | ANDY KISSANE	60
Flannel Flowers | OMAR MUSA	61
FOR GIORGIO | KEN BOLTON	62
43 | ASIEL ADÁN SÁNCHEZ	64
Free Sonnet | JOSIE JOCELYN SUZANNE	67
Garden Dreaming | KIM CHENG BOEY	68
Gunny Sack Rebellion | ELENA GOMEZ	70
The Heart of the Advocate | ANGELA COSTI	72
Hummingbird Country | DEBBIE LIM	73
I have become psychologically linked to a humpback whale | CLAIRE ALBRECHT	75
I want/don't want a place | A FRANCES JOHNSON	77
Landscapes, with Poem | MARJAN MOSSAMMAPARAST	79
Last appointment of the day | KIRWAN HENRY	82
last swim before space flight | RORY GREEN	83
The Last Male White Rhinoceros | NANDI CHINNA	84
Leafless–Leafs | LOUISE CRISP	88
Live from Gaza | SARA M SALEH	89
Losing Alexandria | LENI SHILTON	94
Mandala | BONNY CASSIDY	96
Mandelbrot Set | JENNIFER HARRISON	101
Marshmallow flowers | MITCHELL WELCH	103
Migration | NICOLE JIA MOORE	104
natural history poem | JONATHAN DUNK	105
Notes on the After | DEREK CHAN	106
On Not Cutting Through | BARRY HILL	107
optimal | ALISON WHITTAKER	110

Orphic Elegy V	LUKE FISCHER	114
Penstock Lagoon	SARAH DAY	117
peptalk	JOANNE BURNS	119
Photograph: Sunday with Joy, carrying Sweeney at Heide	EMILIE COLLYER	120
Pikes Peak	SARAH HOLLAND-BATT	122
Poem for my Ancestors	EILEEN CHONG	124
poem for protection	ELLEN VAN NEERVEN	127
The Portable Home	SABA VASEFI	128
prayer for the parents of every addict	SCOTT-PATRICK MITCHELL	130
Pumping Station	ISI UNIKOWSKI	132
Purgatory	JUDITH CRISPIN	134
quandongs	MAYA HODGE	136
Rain	GLENN MCPHERSON	138
recline	DAVID STAVANGER	141
Rendezvous	BROOK EMERY	143
Requiem (fire)	DAVID BROOKS	144
Rezoning	JOHN KINSELLA	146
Rivers	YEENA KIRKBRIGHT	150
Ruby	DR CHELINAY GATES AKA MULARDY	152
The Saltpan	YASMIN SMITH	154
Salt Water Kin	JILL JONES	156
Scar Tissue	ES FOONG	158
Scarred Landscape	BRENDA SAUNDERS	159
Sea Cliff	MARTIN LANGFORD	160
sealed tight for safety	HASIB HOURANI	162
Self-addressed	LESH KARAN	165
Sestina: Pain	STUART BARNES	166
signs from the dead	PANDA WONG	168
something specific about this boodja	NADIA RHOOK	170
Songs you can't hear	TIMMAH BALL	172

still the night parrot sings	JAZZ MONEY	175
Surfacing	MICHELLE CAHILL	177
Surfing Again	SIMONE KING	178
Tabulations (A Nine Year)	GRACE YEE	179
Talara'tingi	FELICITY PLUNKETT	180
Tenebrae	THEODORE ELL	181
Transported	LOU GARCIA-DOLNIK	182
Two Cities	JARAD BRUINSTROOP	152
Watching Adrianne Lenker Play Guitar with a Paintbrush	KRISTIAN RADFORD	184
The Weight of Words	JENA WOODHOUSE	185
The Wolves of Mayo	ANNE WALSH	187
The Yield	EUNICE ANDRADA	190
Your Bones of Glass	DAMEN O'BRIEN	191

Notes on Contributors	193
Guest Editor Biographies	208
Acknowledgements and Publication Details	209

POEMS

*A Poem In Honour Of A Lioness Perfecting Her Balance
Of Inner/Outer Power* | SISTA ZAI ZANDA

Gentleness is her Superpower.
And,
She works it *generous*
But
Just like a Lioness.

See:
Overstep or disrespect and
Soon. You. Will. Learn.

        Yes, she is a Lioness.
        She regally balances

    Supple Softness   And   Agile Fierceness.

    And this delicate balance of power,
        Well, it's rarely welcomed.
        But
        She'll be the first to tell you,
    Ever so gently,
    "Your Fear is none of my business."

Gentleness.   Gentleness.   Gentleness.   Gentleness.
        Gentleness.

    Gentleness is her superpower.
        And she works it, *generous*
        But
        Like a Lioness

> Because she overstands the **Mystery:**
> Her gentleness complements and strengthens
An unapologetic roar and uncompromising defence.
> As the ancients say:
> ***Shumba musango haizi yokutamba.***

Gentleness is her superpower.
And she works it,
Generous
But
Like a Lioness—
So, overstep or disrespect, then
Soon. You. Will. Learn.

> Yes!
> She is a Lioness.

Ableism is the pre-existing condition that puts us at risk*
| ANDY JACKSON

analysts said people had just gotten tired
of being careful   officials say people will die
but we say we aren't dead yet   time
and ventilators are scarce   you have no idea

who might be vulnerable around you   we are

being asked to make enormous, difficult decisions
so that other people can go to the pub   normal
birthed me yet normal wants to extinguish me
    zoom crip dance parties and contact-free baskets

of extra veggies—life saving crip mutual aid survival

    I want to believe that the future is
not just mine but ours   am I scared that the hospital
won't let me in? every single second   when anyone
says it's only the old and unhealthy who are dying

we say stop racist-eugenics now   I write

using *us*, *we* and *our* to represent how this community
is part of me   bad jokes, memes and tacos
count as mutual aid   to not wear a mask is not
an act of freedom—it is callous   it is radical to love

    a body that the world says is wrong

---

* Only the title of the poem is mine. Its words come from (in order) Bri M ("Maybe We Shouldn't Go Back to Normal", *The Nation*, 30 June 2021), Crip Fund, Alice Wong ("I'm Disabled and Need a Ventilator to Live: Am I Expendable in this Pandemic?", *Vox*, 4 April 2020), Anthea Williams ("For Those of Us with Disabilities, Lockdown Won't End as long as Covid Strategies Leave Us Behind", *The Guardian*, 31 December 2021), El Gibbs ("People with Disability 'Completely Overlooked' as Omicron Surges", *SBS News*, 20 December 2021), Bri M, Leah Lakshmi Piepzna-Samarasinha ("How Disabled Mutual Aid is Different than Abled Mutual Aid", *Disability Visibility Project*, 3 October 2021), Alice Wong, Amy Gaeta ("Disabled Communities in the Covid-19 Pandemic", *Disability Visibility Project*, 26 March 2020), Crip Fund, Amy Gaeta, Leah Lakshmi Piepzna-Samarasinha, Anthea Williams, Frances Ryan ("Living in a Woman's Body: this body is a genetic mistake—but it is sex, laughter and beauty too", *The Guardian*, 10 February 2022).

After Franz Marc, The Dreamer (1912) | PETER BOYLE

They are always arriving, the blue horses,
so close they could almost nuzzle
the back of your left ear.
Just when you thought to have done with the world
they are here shimmering from the green meadows
as you sit there cross-legged
but the thighs opened wide
as if to give birth to the dream of yourself.

For so long you'd anticipated something from the receding hills
and the tall thin houses of childhood,
and how many times they must have come unnoticed
when your eyes were glazed over,
swallowed by elsewheres.

And now the roar of the world has stepped away.
Dreamer who speaks with your body,
today you have awoken inside yourself.
May the blue horses guide you forever.

All Markets are All Universes | LIONEL FOGARTY

Universal not own by anybody
Universal food must not be own, by anyone
Universal water must not be owned, by anybody
Trees are reef thirst of every hearts pulse beat
Channels of all first nation got to be relations
Changing all first people, to be what they want won't do;
The cycle of life, all survive by truth quenched by justices.
'Poor will be shops of their own'
The bikes cars bus trams all types are everyone's travel,
When planes fall remember who flyed first without steels.
There is honey in every worlds, don't sip its poisons
Marriage those loves before the communicate.
Many adorable smeared words came from the wrong TV internets
Many agony are fibs by the society, who think they closing us better ha ha
The heart on legs knee the hair of all air
     sound mad, but man made by land has a chance.
Lots of mornings desire joy the sad which nests
Lots stabbed by the top nut on the wheels fast
     slow as if peace is the dark blood moneys.
Remove the worn out old times
Remain our supreme before new world order came
Relive the paradise where the finger are the painters
     maps to the earth unhurt.
Cultures of we native no matter where we are in this worldliness, are to come back
Struggled by battle as to help by are the healed kind vein the good lay sick human being trying to be us as anybody.
The drain of the sewage sometime bring more life in escaping a cage up cell sleeps
Firewood is wealth beyond the stove planner cooked matchmakers.
Landloves are not a city path road only when earth has the right to awaken
     the babies bornunborn.
     Universal Fathers an Mothers send all us the owner of hearts life-falls.
All the markets are all universes

Anyhow Poem | LOUIS KLEE

    for I,
      I
     over-
       whelm over-
whelm into the white flat sea
the white on off-white light, the sea
is a painting nature cannot imitate—
that is, infinite. Meaning sticks to us.
Mules for meaning, bearing meaning, I don't care:
the idea of materialism, the hooligan idea: I don't care.
      That feeling when some singular
        unrelatable feeling when
             when, when
                will this be anything other than it is—
this morning drawing writing—mark-
making, word-work, the tongue
clings thick to my mouth and I sing
Mediterranean hot and lost, an octopus, ocean-
born for bliss. These smudges, leapings,
scatters, and scratches; these smears, thrills,
flourishes, and dashes; scuffs as
ornate as the candelabra. You
sleep in boots and somehow still magnify—loan
me your limousine, boar fur, Vienna
velum with lemon. Bandage my eyes.
I am crying because there are tears in my eyes.
I feed them—I can't help it—
and they coo at morning like broken
plumbing, unused doors, unused silver, god
grant the children easy exams—go out

and get me my shotgun. I'm sorry
to bother you, write that.
Wild alive and willing—no,
wanting—I owe you nothing
but the happy fact we coincide
in this sun slant, defrauding small accidents
that must happen again and again.
Love depends.

Note: 'Anyhow Poem' quotes my own loose translation of a line from Heinrich Heine's *Deutschland. Ein Wintermärchen* (the first two lines of the last stanza in Caput X) and is referring to Anna Mendelssohn's *Implacable Art* with 'loan me your limousine' and 'word-work'. Other more general and imprecise allusions are to Cy Twombly's painting (especially Mary Jacobus' interpretation of these paintings), Wordsworth's *The Prelude* ('willing, nay—nay, wishing'), and Seferis' 'Three Secret Poems'.

Art for art's sake | THUY ON

Those paper cuts
outside of tradition
Pater and Wilde and Swinburne

degenerates in the service of words:
it's not utilitarian not a bridge
your soul will not be higher learned

a poem is not moral fibre
washed down with holy water
taken with a grimace

exempt from the body politic
its charm lies in its charm
an anathema to rectitude

just as Beardsley's curiosities
in those black and white lines
are to be swooned over ecstatically

all art is quite useless
to be lived beautifully
a flower unfurls for itself.

Art That Moves | JESSICA L WILKINSON

Mirka Mora Tram No 243, Melbourne, 1978

i.

Mirka is well-prepared for the vast canvas
of the tram's exterior—her diary displays
lessons drawn from Chevreul, Gage, Berlin
& Kay; her concentrated study of mythology
and histories of art. She stirs *air, mood,
passion* as paint fumes rise from a limited
palette: black for night and white for day,
red most known and green familiar.
Vines skirt the running board and climb
the doorframe, blooming into round red

roses and fable—a bestiary bookended
with locomotive angels. On the inside,
Mirka riffs on Edward Lear, evolves
his nonsense verse for Melbourne accents
and her love of snails: *crawly crawl crawl
crawl*, she has one say in cursive strokes
of rhyme, appealing to the child in all
commuters. Enamel haunts her nose
for days; her arm will be sore for eight
months. Pleasure can be painful work.

ii.

Standing on the corner of Lt. Collins and Swanston
Mirka spies the white moth quavering up the line.
Its wings grow larger and larger, reaching wide
as white unveils her reds and greens; illusions
of yellow, brown and blue. Animals mature
into folk art, a happy charge of fauna on a free
ride through the city. Shop windows rattle and smile.

iii.

Pressed through glass and into fabric
Mirka's musing image folds four decades
on that very corner where she stood—
Gorman® dresses and shirts hold her
angels and serpents, birds and beasts—
made to move and moving still.

Aubade, Allegro | ALEX SKOVRON

'The past is never where you think you left it.'
—Katherine Anne Porter

A line of light from a passing van sweeps the ceiling
like a blade. Something becomes.
The days have tumbled—a snaking row of dominoes,
history in disarray. And then an intrusion
of thought as the zeros clatter their alarum.
You tap the phone, tapping blessed silence. Lately
the gender of trees, the dance of isobars, monuments
shifting and foolish ships colonize
your obsessions. In a sushi parlour you overheard
'Ah, yes, gravitas', and the rhyme wouldn't release you,
its satiric grin. Compulsive, you emailed it
to yourself, let it haunt the inbox unopened,
then a spark spoke up: Time is orthogonal, its walls sheer,
deceptive as glass, and the angles crawl
ever inwards and out, *a meandros* in four dimensions.
But the futility of this conceit washes over you,
sense collapses, and a police helicopter
is shredding the counterfeit quiet. You drift
downstairs—yesterday, where's yesterday? A line from
somewhere: May the end hold memory not misery …

You stop, listen. A piano's rhetoric has been looping
inside your skull: Sonata 18, that glorious leap
into bar 46—and gratitude lifts the hot urn, teaspoon
of brown dust, a quaver of milk. A bird, maybe
Beethoven himself, sweeps the window like a ghost.
You drum the keyboard bench, prepare to perform the day.

'Australianesque' | MICHAEL FARRELL

Peter Porter wrote a sonnet sequence about Christopher Brennan which has never been published. Peter showed me the poem in a notebook, during my brief time as Brian Castro. I didn't feel comfortable being Castro long, although Brian himself was fine with it: particularly given my work with Melbourne's Hong Kong community (giving advice on being gay or queer in Australia, offering practice dating sessions, etc.). The poem had the title 'Australianesque', which Peter verbally qualified as a working one. He was venturing (his verb) on the acrostic form not, à la Gwen Harwood, with any mischievous intent, yet partly in mild homage to her famous stunt. Rather than use, as would be conventional—he felt, he said, too conventional—Brennan's or Harwood's names, he used the fourteen letters of the coinage, 'Australianesque', to start each line. Hence his reservation regarding the title, which would give it away. The poem,

And the notebook itself, seem to have disappeared. I went through Porter's archive—and talked to his lovely daughter—when I was Helen Garner, and had an idea about writing a book about death as emotional blackmail, tentatively titled 'The Ultimate', that would bring Ted Hughes, Brennan, and other male writers together. My (i.e. Helen's) publisher was sceptical, and the project died a natural death. By then I was myself again. It's a funny position to be in, when my own interests overlap with those of the identities I assume. I write poems about the quarrels I have with myself—usually to do with approach, and emphasis—like a proper Yeatsian, and wish I could talk to (or as?) Judith Wright about them. Peter Steele writes about this notion somewhere; but Peter P never mentioned Yeats to me. He seems livelier than W.B. Perhaps we could compare Yeatsians with Steinian poets, along the lines of a quarrel with nouns? But not here. I remember

The poem itself better than others that I've been shown
by my illustrious antecedents, because of the form. E.g. N for
Ned Kelly. In the poem, he appears as Brennan's spiritual ancestor. Or
perhaps rhetorical ancestor's more accurate. Compare Kelly's
Jerilderie Letter to Brennan's *Musicopoematographoscope* and I think
you will see what I mean. It's the productive convergence
of a desperation to be heard, coupled with an enraged desire to damn
their respective audiences. If it's tempting to wonder what Porter's
brilliant mind might've done with I for Indigenous or Q for Queer, that
is to wonder like a person of 2021 or -22. You can spell 'Australian-
esque' without other key initials: G for Gold, M for Migrant, C for
Convict (e.g.). Porter was, rather, I think, interested in the vague,
philosophical, slipperiness of the suffix '-esque' (including both
'Dantesque' and 'carnivalesque' in his poem): its shortfall, its excess.

The Bees | CLAIRE POTTER

There was a   hum of   fretwork   guess-
work   a piecework of selves   on the veranda   where I asked
my mother   *how much did it cost   to carry   so many filaments
two instead of one*   when smocked   and behoved
                  we left the hospital   each with a   different
kind of insomnia——a different kind
                          of question   and a
different kind of   mother   torn under a yolk
                                    of glistening sun
that put everything   on the table   whether
                we wished it or not

      In the late summer   a kind of lull   sulked around
the house   not deliberately   but everybody unconsciously
slowed their blood   assumed the right position   even visitors
——children knew to play outdoors while adults
              continued to plait bread   and vacuum

When mulberries finished flexing   their purplish seeds
a more ancient time arrived   and out of silence I   remember
   climbing through a wall of thorny scrub
      to find a tree   in a clearing
swathed in bees   and at the heart   a black sun into which all
     bees travelled   Here I put my sibling
and   my mother's caul of tears   into a pollen pot that swayed
   in step with the wind   It was no altar
           but a cup of   gold-dusted slumber   that stung and over-
swarmed   with a dissident task——irrational
    plentiful
                bristling with relief——stoic as moon-
light unearthed from   the ash   of sleep

Being My Grandmothers (After Uluru*)
| JENNIFER KEMARRE MARTINIELLO OAM

I recovered a reverberation of sounds from the rocks/the red earth/from the
paleo river scars/from the beaches like *Kamay* ** … half-buried in the quicksand

of forgetfulness …half-disinterred to be rematriated like Ancestral remains
ancient in-my-blood sounds/lost/taken under the blanket suffocations of colonial

history for unheard/unheeded yet enduring un-muffled echoing …
in my children's throats/in my grandchildren's throats/whispering/singing

resurrecting an archaeology of lost sounds/the first ceremonies/ the first
lullabies/hunting songs and whale songs/laughter and healing songs

Creation stories and True Stories/a heritage of grandmothers' voices
millennia long speaking with Uluru's… a genealogy of words/once spoken/forever

echoing in my throat/in my children's throats/in my grandchildren's throats…
I retrieved a broken word today, picked it up off the ground where it had been

thrown away/carelessly like an empty plastic bottle/a bit crushed like an utterance
might crack with emotion between a vowel and a consonant of a word once

meant to be whole/a container of meaning and substance/integrity to sustain
futures like water might quench drought and thirst/nourish and give life but can't
because

someone who didn't know/didn't understand/didn't respect this place/ this Law
thought it wasn't relevant/that it didn't have a use/a meaning /a place thought

it didn't belong same way they didn't belong to this place/where words are sacred/
are covenants/not defiled/dismembered/re-purposed for political convenience

I heard a bloodless sound after Uluru/a string of words like stones bereft
of spirit/heart/life/without skin or pulse to render its speakers worthy of belonging/

worthy to be keepers of the Rule of Law...
denial is a chasm two and a half centuries deep/the wound-salted erosion

of the land/of our bodies/of our soul/the induced deprivation of an ecology where
'absence' and 'truth' occur in the same sentence without parole or redemption

* The Uluru Statement: Voice, Treaty, Truth
** Eora name for Botany Bay

Blame the Greenies | CATH DRAKE

If they hadn't dressed like hippies. Didn't talk
mumbo jumbo one love. Hadn't shunned suits.
Catastrophised too early. If they hadn't done those

twirling fire stick dances. Looked too happy. Too
radical. Had so many piercings. Grew dreadlocks.
Presumed they were superior. Kept telling us

what to do. Been anti-progress, anti-good times.
Wanted to ban everything. Hung around in crowds.
Failed university. Slept in. Partied all the time and if

they hadn't been so middle class. Mainstream.
Out of touch. So finger-pointing smug. Puritanical
Fantasists! Noisy. Made everything into a problem—

argumentative. If they hadn't been hysterical. Bleak.
Stubborn. Blocked roads. Got arrested. Refused
to have children. If they'd *just* been more honest.

Hadn't produced so many dull reports. Talked
jargon. Been too quiet. Too small in number to be
useful. If they hadn't marginalised themselves.

Been covert. Driven cars. So hypocritical. Picked on
the wrong people. At the wrong time. If they hadn't been
anti-science. Rejected proper jobs: MPs or CEOs!

Been so naïve. Irrational. If they hadn't been useless
at planning. Smoked too much. Given up easily. Tasted
the good life. Got trendy. Or too darn sensible. If they

hadn't got older, had families, full-on careers. Been selfish.
Weak willed. Complicated. Wanted to do things their way.
Impractical. If they'd just been *much* smarter. And *why*

didn't they just get Bieber and Beyoncé involved.
Branson and Musk. If they hadn't been so brazen,
coming right up to us and telling us straight in our faces.

book of hours | HARRY REID

this is the poem from my dream I say / office hours are a myth / publishing poems is money for nothing / the supermarket is both under and over policed / today the first thing I said was 'shut up' (cat) / possible upsides to a pandemic include the death of musicals / possible downsides include the personal essay / publishing poems is printing money but the money is bad / I've found this year that I'm a betting man / you could chase me down the street but where would I go / I'd like to write a poem in the style of 'Scott 4' / but how can you / maybe only via legacy / don't trust the morning to do the evening's work / I am absolved by my position at the desk / I am freed by my duty of care / publishing poems is money in the bank / reading poems is time off the clock / my afternoon is my employer's / my fingers are my own / who dictates the roll economy / 2 kids = time off in lieu / turn poetry into stocks / by sitting here I am winning / I am luckier than most / there are no doubt those who would kill for this mousepad / but does the reverse apply / two-factor authentication is a misnomer / there are three factors and the third is yourself / your desire to log in / possible upsides to working from home include increased productivity / possible downsides include lockable doors / work in its purest form is art / labour in essence is love / I am forgiven by my reputation as an entrepreneurial spirit / of what I'm still unsure / today outside is ferocious / ulcers are mysterious with none of mystery's romance / no-one 'gets' the shop anymore / are personal printers 'back' or 'out' / the only conscionable thing is to have nothing to show for a week's work & a blank cv / in what way are we trending / could we get a report on that / I am still a young man / I am making a difference / up the garden path is still a viable pathway / being here negates the possibility of being there / publishing poems looks good on a resume / can we push our 2 to 4 / our 4 to tomorrow / ergonomics can be a spiritual practice if you let it / plants are an acceptable worry / there is nothing more interesting than weather / to buy a scanner is to understand Marx's theory of the commodity / to send a fax is to understand purity / possible upsides to a volatile market include a sense of adventure / possible downsides include losing everything / by taking up this space I am useful / my presence is internally monetised / what appears to be a choice is often no choice at all / for example: ink / by writing this poem I am 'taking back' / but the poem is only anti-capital when secret / this is good for employers / a clean desk is a happy desk / I am driven by my tendency to help / a problem shared is the terrain of the consultant / a problem halved is one of countless outcomes / would it be more tedious to stop or continue / do you archive or remember / how to measure ethics on a matrix / the modern office is post-cubicle / friday is losing its cultural relevance / if you're never really 'on' you can never really be 'off' / I am on track to meet my goals / this provides some comfort / the colour of a lanyard can tell you everything / this office block is over 100 years old / but what of the soil beneath that / or beneath that again / a good worker has a clear trajectory / often this requires obstacles to be cleared / I am embarking on a new chapter / I am realigning my values / Heraclitus' theory of the break room / HR's theory of culture / publishing poems is an act of inflation / a sunny day has economic implications / a clear commute is a glimpse at divinity / morale is a budgetable cost / possible upsides to a restructure include increased efficiency / possible downsides include clearing your desk / this is the poem from my dream I say / a good worker is like a tree / inherently removable

Briefly on the Mountain | KRISTEN LANG

The human I live with
is across the water, holding the hand
    of his father who is dying—

I and the dog
we slip into calling 'ours'
    are here, under the mountain.

And maybe place
is never really the contour but the climb,
    the steepness pressing the touch

into time
the body remembers. His father moans
    against the pain, against

the pain killers, wanting
some other plateau, a pulse more
    ocean

than his own, more
air and thrum than lying
    in the fade of his warmth.

I want his son
this same way—the litheness
    of the river, the depth of stone,

the wrinkled tree stoic on the paths
of my walking. To know
    his weather through my own,

the tangle of us
under the wind-shaped branches of the forest.
    We are distracted

by the self. This moment reminding us
the hour is still arriving—death
    comes / goes. He calls me now,

asks how I am, says
barely anything, relief   slow-danced
    in the arms of loss.

The dog and I step
into moonlight, the blue-white stones
    of the mountain

drifting into the night. How the horizon
is just a game, the son, like the dog,
    spinning towards the day a while,

my pulse
brushed by the falling
    of its rain.

buried light | ALISON J BARTON

next to bones
what ledger of curiosity
brought ghosts to this land
funerals to these sites
and lulled us to grief?

we wore trauma on our sleeves
and looked lived in
we blacked moths at sunrise
our deaths writ large
imagined in the
dark buried in the wild

we were bound by an era
by registers of speech
we made the shape of eagles
with our hands
and summoned our injuries
to the light

we spoke with foreign mouths
as if burying light
with hackneyed blades

by rough white skies
we found ancestors together
in our talk
injected ourselves with
the impression of spirits

afloat in a cold haze
the silver underside of a
shrub bristled the bank
lit the thin of our ice skin

resting in the water
over family family family sand prints
we watched silently
not worrying on future catastrophes
there was to be no congregation
that year

where will we go after this
  caught by the hair of a skull
  the scalp of a neck
  backbone bold
waiting for the sun to
settle the torture in us all

a burned-down hut
will be too cold to tell
it grows plants in you,
but does not fill noble feet with instinct

tell me your experience of losing a home
of light on a dark sound
of a cliff-face invisible in the dawn
of the privileged many

we will leave this house
we are mist along the walls

Buzz Words | ANN VICKERY

Now more than ever, workers downgraded as non-essential pivot from WTF to WFH. Sartre or the state redefine the family covidiot, rejecting iso and loving Nietzsche's herd immunity. Unprecedented intimacy heightens the need to test and trace close contacts. Amid the storm, we curate content, hoping to prepone concerns and disambiguate human capital. This is the new normal in the time of COVID. Reach out and circle back, the media monsters teen spirit with fake news. Emergency management clamps down on border loves while we recount stimulus packages. Some days you decide not to dial back in. On-shoring the inadequate message: we're all in this together. Going forward then two steps back. Getting back to business in these uncertain times.

Canticle for a Dancing Man | STEPHEN GILFEDDER

It has come to this, the embalmed fifties
Flat is all that's left for my declining friend,
After eight years still mourning a lost love,
In half-light, half-blind, drinking vodka
From late morning, all skin and bone
Among his treasures, traymobiles, valve radios,
Boat shoes on, drapes closed against the day.

Half a lung removed, a personal trainer comes
Daily, needs aerobics now to make the stairs.
In other times he danced on tabletops
In Turkish slippers, roamed bathhouses hidden
Down blind alleys, rowed shimmering tides
Stripped to the waist, singlet balled in the prow,
Ghostly crews left haunting hallway walls.

Over the same ground always, stories
Ballooning in implication with repetition.
Nothing left to say, I leave him, anchorite,
Not knowing where we go from here
Framed at the door among polystyrene boxes
From the Council, scrawled delivery notes,
Pharmacy receipts, empties from the liquor stash.

Walls outside carry messages from beyond,
Tagged hieroglyphs alive with cartoon faces
That could be us, rendered to a demotic script.
Heaven sent, a local shaman has come to bless
The scene, weaving towards me, holding forth
To one and all, arguing with himself, skipping down
The street crab-wise, showing some sort of way.

Case # 70 | SAMAH SABAWI

This is not how I imagined it would be
Legs parted on the blood-soaked dirt
Strangers rolling up my skirt
Hands pulling down my undies
UN observers counting indignities
They write me down
They write me down
They write me down a number
I'm case # 70

I inhale the wisdom of a thousand matriarchs
And the patience of a million refugees
I exhale fear and tyranny
I'm not a stray animal abandoned by the roadside
That ambulance is here for me
I booked a hospital room
I decorated a nursery
I even prepared a music playlist
To reduce my anxiety
But all of this is out of reach
I'm case # 70

Guns loaded
Phones shooting
Can I have some privacy?
I inhale the scent of lemon
The fragrance of jasmine
The warmth of your skin
The tenderness of your flesh
Finally slipping out of me

And into a spectacle of inhumanity
I exhale tears and anger
This is snot how I imagined it would be
I'm case # 70

I breathe you in
And breathe everything out
Until you and I are all there is
And all there is ... is you and me
We're case # 70

Choice Cuts | MYKAELA SAUNDERS

I got a bone to pick with capitalism—and a few to break.
— Refused, 'Worms of the Senses / Faculties of the Skull'

my blood is worth bottling, so I'm told   as though
                                                       I'm made of gold

                as if I'm worth my weight in clinking coins—

        but I tiptoe around this auctioneer's fairground, quietly,
        acting as though there's nothing of value inside me

cos all these sly salespeople size me up like this is a meat market
fetishised flesh up for auction, or slaughter
sleazy leers that weigh me and measure me   butcher me

                                I've seen the gleam on every licked lip
                                concealing carving knife tongues

lifetime of little remarks mark and re-mark me

I got thick skin but it's no good thing—scar tissue as sensitive as tough—
maladaptive trait from poking and prodding
and wondering and weighing
my blood against their knowledge
of a curated culture—a pale imitation of what lives and breathes—
concocted by experts in ivory towers,
                        published in papers without our permission,
                        bound up in books we can't afford to read,
                        sermonised by grifters inside stolen sandstone walls
under whose scrutiny
I WANT TO MUTINY

                                I scrunch myself up like waste paper instead

and chew on life-long meditations, like:

    —how to lease my labour in balance, with dignity
    within a market monetising indignity and imbalance

                              —how to talk about my culture
                                    without the vultures
                                  descending on my words,
                            to pick and flick and peel and pull
                          so the sores just keep on weeping

    —how to say the things I-need-to-but-shouldn't
    or they'll attract wights like flies,
    like feral camp dogs
    sniffing round and humping the corpses of my ancestors

                            —how to hold onto my integrity
                  when cold neoliberal logic drills into me
and the colonial vacuum sucks the marrow from me as fodder

I want to be sustained but the terms are extractive
    for an early casualty of late-stage capital,
        dreaming dead desires—

                      mobility

            upward   through

      of   trickle-

                                  down

                                      economics

this pyramid schema is not so classy,
reducing us all to fucking tiers
& if I don't laugh I'll cry

        poor me!

                    I'd sell my soul to speak a language
                       that doesn't commodify the sacred
                 or express despair and disdain in economic frames

                            but here I am—

speaking words that colonised our old people's tongues
same time their babies and wages were stolen

                            bit rich!

                    (well. Uncle David's on the fifty dollar note now
                     but I never get to look at his face for too long)

        no free rides here
        the only inheritance I'll ever get
        is all this trans-generational baggage I never wanted

and these precious bones get heavy
and when you're poor—can't eat or dream—
all you wanna do is slip a femur from your thigh
pop it out the way a black bean slips its skin
crack him clean open, pour
the bright rich marrow
into a bowl
and offer it
to whoever is sniffing around

                            for a meal ticket
                                            or even just a meal

Cicadas | DIMITRA HARVEY

Spring unrolled skies like runners of pink muslin, breezes
steeped in honeycomb. Set out flowers in pastry

blues and glacé reds; summer simmered at the season's
edge, began to smoke. That's when I found their shells

everywhere—like pods of blown sugar, trimmed
to the trunks of bloodwoods, blue gums.
*
Yolk light streaked tower windows. Down Dixon Street,
the grills hissed, spitting oil. Plane trees offered their leaves
to the pavement in helpings of ginger and oxblood. I watched

strangers champ down fists of minced squid, or tighten
the nooses of their scarves, as lanterns swung
like pomelos from the eaves of tea rooms, and the dusk

slung up its meathook moon. This was Chinatown
on a Friday night—the markets packed. The scent of burning sugar
lured me from my mother to a stall where toffee

oozed in an iron pot. A woman was rolling
a knot of it to a worm. She jutted one end in her mouth
and blew; and as the sugar ballooned, she began

pinching and pulling it, shaping wings, a square
jaw, a long torso coiling round itself—all the while
filling it with her breath, as if creation were a kind of

mouth to mouth—then she took the end from her lips
and tweaked it shut. Deft as a doctor's
stitch she embedded a skewer, tilted the dragon

towards light so it shimmered, copper-bronze.
I watched as she made a horse, a rat—my tongue watering,
even though I knew they were not for eating.
*

Now rummaging at weeds on my knees
in the veggie beds, my fingers scrape the crisp
toffee abdomens of cicada shells. I press aside
drooping leaves of eggplants—the fat fruits,

black as hearses, nodding, glinting offhandedly.
I pull oxalis, dandelion from their roots. Throw
the first in a pile for the worms, heap
the latter by my knee for later:
*

Stir eggs and dill, diced shallots, grated feta and kefalograviera
until combined. Add a dash of olive oil, salt. Fold-in diced
chard and the wild greens you pulled from the hedgerow, the side
of the road—like the peasant grandmother who lived through famine
and three wars, raised twenty children, and knew that everywhere

the earth makes offerings of nourishment. Line your cooking tin
with pastry thin and pale as a cotton shroud. Anoint with olive oil. Now
spoon the mixture evenly across your tray and cover with more pastry.
Puncture the top with a fork or skewer—so steam—like the soul
through the mouth at death—can escape. Cook till golden.
*

For weeks, the air throbbed with their love songs, their
jackhammer dirges, as they bred and died, became banquet
for lizard and bird. I've imagined that moment of revelation:
seventeen years tucked in the dirt, sucking root sap, then—

the sudden insistent urge to burrow up and out… Exposed
to light and the swiftness of air for the first time, the old self
ruptures, peeling back—wings unfurl, silent
gossamer. Sometimes I find one, the shell

not entirely sloughed, the crisp, veined wings only
partly unfolded. My eyes track the conveyor belts
of ants: they till the corpse, ferry
morsels to the nest.
*
I ready the ground for sowing. Swing the mattock round again,
tear up another sod. A butcherbird probes the edges of opened

earth and plucks up worms purple-red as sopressa. Skinks

tongue crickets by the irrigation runnels. A kookaburra drops
from the shed then wings north—a marsh snake thrashing

in its beak. Above rotted orange peels, celery tufts, the skins

of pumpkins heaped on the compost—fruit flies hover like tossed
confetti. Westering now, the sun spills her brandy down

the hills; mosquitoes bore for my veins's hard liquor.

Closet Monster | SAMUEL WAGAN WATSON

A splice of a sweet trumpet... the fractured edge from a mellow ska-riff ...
    'Do you remember the good old days before the ghost town?
SCRATCH! DISTORTION! FEEDBACK! CLICK!
    'Do you remember the good old days before the ghost town?'
A splice of a sweet trumpet... the fractured edge from a mellow ska-riff....

Sad, old, Grover Finlay collapsed into his dead mother's bed... cheap white wine spiriting his feeble mind... deleting caution... an early kookaburra breaking dawn with mocking laughter... interrupted by the woeful waning cries of a death bird; curlew lurking in nearby mangroves on the river... and sad, old, Grover Finlay - ..an elderly Aboriginal man... living alone and intoxicated... commencing the REMs of buzz-saw sleep apnea... without a notice that he had neglected to securely shut the warped door of his dead mother's closet... a pair yellow eyes, like the spectres of ectoplasmic urine, scanning the slumber of sad, old, Grover Finlay...

A splice of a sweet trumpet... the fractured edge from a mellow ska-riff...
'Do you remember the good old days before the ghost town?'
SCRATCH! DISTORTION! FEEDBACK! CLICK!
'Do you remember the good old days before the ghost town?'
A splice of a sweet trumpet... the fractured edge from a mellow ska-riff

Sad, old, Grover Finlay collapsed into his dead mother's bed ... cheap white wine spiriting his feeble mind ... deleting caution ... sad, old, Graver Finlay... he was off-guard and unaware ... caught in horrors mire, as he tired, forgot to close up everything when he expir ... the eyes in the closet, yellow and septic, like the spectres of ectoplasmic urine, stared at him as an edition of a 1981, 12 inch .45 of The Specials played stuck, almost morosely .. stylus skipping in a portable vintage phono-case on the bedroom bureau ... and the eyes, t eyes that no amount of early morning mist could disguise, biding its evil time over the innocent but sad old, Grover Finlay,..

A splice of a sweet trumpet… the fractured edge from a mellow ska-riff…
'Do you remember the good old days before the ghost town'
SCRATCH! DISTORTION! FEEDBACK! CLICK!
'Do you remember the good old days before the ghost town?
A splice of a sweet trumpet… the fractured edge from a mellow ska-riff…

The police report would later say that the 68-year-old Indigenous man was intoxicated when He died… cause of death was due to asphyxiation/asphyxiaphilia with a woman's stocking… Groverly Finlay had been working on his unsolicited manuscript of poetry, entitled: 'MONSTER IN THE CLOSET'…

Coast banksia | ANNE ELVEY

1

they buckle at bent
elbow and   gnarl
silver-sided tongues

slender toward
gravity   upward
are   green surface

to ceiling   their
triple type
of cone   at seed

bristle and bloom are
built   as knack
they bank on sand

send search
for wet   anchor
appointment

and duration   if
later a limb
shears   falls

or wood   one day
welcomes flame
to   step down

gristle of bole   then
can whiskers declare
for   hollowing

2

a tremor of limb
tail   twitches
discernible habit

of host   as aloof
a kind of lumber
as if gait   were

boldened both
and stopped in stone
boots   with sand

at toe and feet
not lead but fibrous
tendrils   why not

say   roots
should this convey
too much of ancestry

impossible to forego
a species' cliché
humankind as   tree

hyphen the others
as bare bend
to motion   survival

brings the amber
of   a world
assumed

3

a seed's scrape
bursts   from pod
absences curve

inside a woody
shell   packed like
text before bristle

yields to   wing
scale   to scud
on this path

littered with twig and
tempt   anticipation
of strangers   keys

in hand when every
tactic taught
is useless   probable

harm becomes
bread   honey
a full moon

invisible   by day
a cone crammed
with   closed cups

its weight on a palm
fist   round the fit
of a thing

'COVID' | GAVIN YUAN GAO

mutters the white man in the whole
-food aisle: cue his scratched-vinyl
voice: cue the leering skull
inked on his arm staring straight
out of two blackholes
through your yellow-peril soul
and you're the devil who's out spreading
his sick of sin in this cut-paper town tonight.

Go home and die, you dirty chink. An extra dose
of reassurance just in case you haven't heard
enough. What's not to love? This
outlaw country that wants you dead each day
but not dead enough to be absolved
of your crime of still breathing
& trying to cling to the incandescent
cadence of your heart.

In the floodlit church
of the supermarket, on this dog-eared
& rain-beaten evening, you stand aflame
like an origin story no one wants
to hear, a chink in the chainmail armour
of a history shining with the fiery
scherzo of poppies & gold-plaqued names
of colonial heroes. You touch the blue

plastic bag of long-grained rice
and think of terraced paddies in Sichuan
gleaming with their silver tresses
of ripening seeds that thrash in the sun
like your grandmother's plaited hair. A lineage

braided & unbraided. You stroke the green corsage
of a bok choy and think of kin, of

blood history, of how the skein of vein throbbed
under Grandma's wrist like a slight, fearless
tremor of earth. 'Covid-19 China Die' was
spray-painted on the garage door of one
Chinese family in Victoria.

What's not to love here?
One yellow body = an entire land
of brown earth where the wind lingers
in fine strokes of hieroglyphs and the swaying
bamboo stalks talk in pentatonic
scales of flute & zither.

And the rumour they've heard is all
true: you breathe through your chink-in-the-wall
your chink-in-the-curtain mouth
and out comes the rice-paper moon
Li Bo wrote about as he lay among
a bed of peonies fifteen centuries ago, drunk
on sweet plum wine & the old grief
of unassuageable loss.

And you alone tonight are China
gleaming with harvest. You, alone, are Li Bo
drunk on grief. You alone are the Chinese moon
drifting through aisles promising
deliverance & plenitude
lifting the light pouring from above
to your burning lips
and you drink.

Crowning | CAITLIN MALING

i.

This is not the beginning
but the view from the window:
a day less glassy-eyed
than I.
      Last day human singular.
The outpouring of waters—
verification of gush
not trickle—

but the drought is tectonic:
plates of orange red rubble
on the rooftop garden
where only crows walk
above a shattered
rainbow of cars

ii.

In our new car
we debate the vaccine,
driving over puddles
that growl red from our paintwork.

I am somewhere in between
the first and second stages
of contractions; this is
a contained enormity

and all life, a vaccine
is a tinge, but, even then,

the virus itself hovers
like the leaf let go

still green with chlorophyll
not yet again the dirt

iii.

Before being returned to dirt
a woman I never forgot told me
a willy wagtail in the house
foretold a death,
she told me their name (djitti djitti)
the clicks they make
when they walk and twitch
towards song but do not sing,
a sound more like your heartbeat
than hooves or the iamb
with its soft breath.
If you are the bird
then I am the house
rafters all

iv.

After all, Rilke never had to make a life.
Grow one. He was visited
by the immaterial,
Angels, he called them,
and also moved inordinately
by statues, bloodless,

without even the flesh
of terra cotta.
          What a thing it is
to have my blood swell like a king tide,
holding you against the shore of my ribs,
a murky clay form
not waiting for signature
or even its own scrawled name.

v.

The chart has my scrawled name.
I have never been one for pain
I keep still and ignore
how it spreads: the twinges
down my legs, sharpening
at the side of my belly out.

Once I read of a poet still writing
though every word
was like casting a stone at himself
directly where others had already landed.

My only poetic secret
is ease, even though the branches
look twisted, they, still, inexorably,
can be followed to light

vi.

I try to follow, light,
to thin and recede,

move away from
self, a face unseen.
'70s mirrors
at the end of poles,
a candle to illustrate

(Remember, she says, no one can make you do anything you don't want to do)

And here are things
I have no desire to see,
the pupil dilated,
even now, the iris
a thin rim of colour
moving back

vii.

Moving back, I imagine my mother
herself bound down by my body;
my grandmother: six children
outlived by five, outliving
her marriage (my grandfather lives on
happily in his third wife with three extra
children to show for it)

My husband, one of one,
parents of one marriage,
children of people
who died still loving
or at least tolerating
one another. My mother-in-law says
this is how is should be

viii.

But this is how it should be:
no skeletal family tree,
you moving through soil
laterally, running like a drain

that keeps the surface parallel
you meet another,
you intersect for a moment
you are stationary

then—you open, continue,

you don't know how many
have passed the green
before it threads

through you
and keeps moving

ix.

They keep me moving
but you do not budge,
asynclitic, your head in my hip
like a semi-colon tying two phrases
together. One inserts a hand
twists, you turn back,
another tries, confirms your stubbornness.
Thirty hours and we are rolled

to another room. I refuse the mirror
held to see the cuts, refuse
even the gap in the covering sheets.
They say it will feel like a tug,
a prying loose and I am a window
frame being lightened of glass

x.

The beginning, a frame
still green with chlorophyll
holding up the rafters,
not waiting for a name,
following light
and moving back,
this is how it should be,
keep moving
lighter than the glass

form you will outlast,
the years flowing
from you like song,
hooves on soft sand
or numbered heartbeats

Death by Vertigo | DAKOTA FEIRER

The Killing Times have ended
so say the books I've read.

Though windows watched apocalypse,
recorded moments in social posts.

Until glass cracked like country roads,
and melted like highway signposts.

A child's eyes bathed in wildfire
grows fear in adult minds.

Scrolling through our species
undeserving of love or virality.

Unlearning their true story,
yearning to be sung again.

Information seems an abyss
of numbness. Carted around in pockets.

Our care now also dwindles.
On cliff edge of news fatigue.

Joining the livestream
of endangered species.

Desacralised in a thirsting ember
of shorthand violence - media cycles.

Third eyes are blinded
by burn marks and blue light.

Burnt carcasses wired
on our coat of arms.

Our totems wailing,
those unburnt lost in haze.

Anthro-gaze is failing
generations proceeding us.

The unborn pleading:
  Please stop her bleeding.

  Please tend to bandaging
  your nationhood's fragility.

  Please consider our inheritance,
  our now lifeless Country.

To heal a corrupt legacy,
we weave with finger and reed.

Baskets, hands, poetry and opinion piece.
Listen. Breathe. Firestick. Drying Leaves.

Through necessity
we must re-pattern.

Rematriate our love
for the Mother.

Together deradicalise love crimes,
like protecting birthing trees.

Learn the plight of our waters.
Listen close to fish screams.

Cleansing a stinking silence,
that reeks across riverbeds.

The Killing Times are of the past,
so the journos have said.

Distrusting them, I consult the stars:
When will the birthing times commence?

The Earwig | AUDREY MOLLOY

1.

At Fethard-on-Sea, in the barrack-
bare dorm, I wake to a scuffling sound
like a mouse in a panel-board wall.
The racket comes from inside my head.
Alarm flushes in, fills my cisterns
with fear that an earwig is piercing
the drum of my ear—translucent and
thin as a Japanese paper door,
past machinations, sound forged from air,

2.

through the labyrinth route to my brain;
that it will chew through, no, *lap up* the
tofu skeins of my temporal lobe,
leaving an airy and honeycombed
bore the breadth of a pair of leather
forewings; that my faculties switch off
in succession like streetlights at dawn:
first, the use of extremities, then
my blink reflex—corneas hardening

3.

like quick-drying glue, my five senses
cauterized, numb to the rasp of sheets
on my knees, stone deaf to my roommates'
idle breath, my tongue a sea slug, dumb
to the pressing need for *help* and *please*,
but a scream is flung, and my eyes (still
oddly shiny) spy the legs of a
girl swinging down from the rim of her
bunk-bed like two links of white pudding—

4.

her Patrick Swayze tee-shirt, her plait
falling over her shoulder as she
rouses the others from sleep—and I
hear, above internal burrowing,
the pounding of bare feet on tile, and
my own racing heart as they carry
me to the day-bright shower block where
the tee-shirted girl advances in
sumo-crouch as though I were rabid,

5.

brandishing two Kirby grips—loosened
from each of her temples—which she moves
like batons to a silent battle-
song, and I know, in some deep (as-yet
un-sacked) silo of my mind, that her
utensils will crush the invader
still deeper and, when withdrawn, will be
coated white and grey; and I hold her
at bay—succeeding through having long

6.

arms—and I scream, this time, for *oil, oil,*
and the sleep-addled teacher arrives,
dragged by one hand, tight in the other
a loden-green bottle, and I watch—
as though from the pebble-dash ceiling—
how I'm laid on my side on the tiles,
how they pour oil in my ear, careful,
ready to scatter, as though it were
water poured into acid, how the

7.

room goes silent, the volume of shrieks
judged by the hands that fly to red-and-
navy mouths, as first the forceps of
the insect's rear emerges and then
the creature, the great queen herself, in
all her plastic-brown entirety,
is free, momentarily, from the
ear, but trapped in the surface tension
of a droplet, prevented from flight

8.

as a woman's heel comes pinkly down
and whitish innards smear and float in
greeny-gold like crushed garlic, the wings
like smashed garlic skin; and how we crawl
back in our bunks and try to sleep, each
with wads of tissue stuffed in our ears,
believing we will never sleep, yet
oversleeping, deaf to the pips of
the eight-o'clock news the next morning.

9.

In years to come, whenever I fail
to summon a person's name or place
I once knew but cannot bring to mind,
I'll think of all the eggs she must have
laid, my tiny one-night stand, the pin-
head pearls she left behind, and how, no
matter how you pound the heel or turn
the wings to skin, you cannot fully
kill a thing that's occupied your mind.

Elephant Rocks | RENEÉ PETTITT-SCHIPP

To reach the beach we must pass through history
the pressure of it, billow of boulders high overhead
            surge of Southern Ocean rising to knees
                      stealing in swift as a thief

we arrive, passage opening to sky
to stand stunned in *Djeran's* crystalline light
towels still wedged under armpits, shoes held in our hands

from translucence the grand monoliths rise
            each a narrative unearthed; violent acts
                of upheaval and molten births
it makes our lives read differently, dwarfed
by geology we do not know but understand
            white sand spilling perfection
                out into the blue-green bay
                  where a herd of elephants—
                      feldspar and alkali, quartz and sanidine
                        make their slow way back out to sea.

Entanglement | TOBY FITCH

I am watching myself untangle
my earphones, my body's walk paused,
standing on the corner of Bedford and Probert
beneath mini grotesques on the roof
of a white and grey self-renovated house,
its ghost gum swaying in the wind
as three trains careen by from different origins,
interlocking like snaking blocks of *Tetris*,
the passengers on board watching my body
standing there on the corner of Probert,
its fingers untangling earphones,
its eyes fixed on a missing parrot poster
taped to a telegraph pole, mind fixating on whether
the silk shirt they're wearing (white feathers
on black) expresses their gender today,
standing on the corner of Probert, sun splitting
the clouds as a gap opens up between trains
permitting past and future to collide,
I am watching myself untangle my earphones
from the roof with the mini grotesques I crouch beside,
ghost gum convulsing in the wind, silver leaves
within reach but obscuring the vermilion
and forest-green parrot whose clipped wings
have carried it from Lilyfield to Newtown,
one dry urban tree to the next, and into my garden
from which I've climbed to the rooftops
in pursuit of the missing bird
whose family has arrived to shout advice
from the street, along with two firemen,
some neighbours and passers-by as three trains

speed to separate destinations, interlocking
like snaking blocks of *Tetris*, my body spaced out
across lightweight tin roof, mind fixating
on whether I am capable of holding this creature
who doesn't want to be held, sweat dripping all the way
to the sidewalk, sun splitting the clouds as a gap
opens up between trains, synapses tethered
to the silver leaves, the wild expectations of the street,
the vermilion and green blur as the parrot slips
my grasp, glides out across Bedford,
just clearing the fence to the train tracks,
clipped wings flapping but not rising,
the thud of its body audible over the screech
of metal on metal, the bright bird
feathered on the dark rocks of the tracks,
face up to the sky, for days to come,
I am watching myself untangle.

Extracts | SUZI MEZEI

Under clammy loam   past the roots
of Bodhi trees, in a place the ancestors
named Colombo
          lie the bones from which
we came, you and I.   Think of the mariner gone
two centuries, stowed in the damp of someone else's
gouged earth, landlocked for eternity,
the owners of the place where he disembarked
                            hurling dirt
on the change he'd brought, gathered like dark pillars
                              on the fringe
of a Christian burial for a tragic Billy Budd,
our great, great, great, etcetera, all bravado
and natural curiosity, a genealogist's conundrum;
his legend mocks documentation, his archaic sextant
condemned to a musty life   in the sea-bitten tea chest
that adorns your mantlepiece, a salt-damaged relic of
expired wanderlust. Think of his marrow, small red specks
dotting the verdant fringe of Negombo,   the nucleotides
that grew our generations. Imagine our long-expired grandmothers
who landed swan-necked, vulnerable as seabirds on the docks,
to marry, to cobble nests among the jam fruit trees, to dodge
cobras; the scrape of coral reef on merchant hulls, their rite
of passage.   Unmoored now, we roll like egret eggs,
you and   I, in different directions,
                                  far from the sea;
the art of navigation sunk within, dormant, unfathomable,
the distance between us, vast.

Family mathematics | TRICIA DEARBORN

But now the huge trick: continued fractions allow you to go on forever, with infinite nesting, just as we allow infinite decimals to go on forever.

—Marty Ross, mathematician

i. Nest

if you're talking children
and ordinals
I was 1st

if you're talking
children and fractions
1 in 4

if you look just at girls
it was 1 in 2

if each unit in a family
is given equal value
1 in 6

not that we were

reality was rationed out
to the powerful

which generates complex equations
hides the damage

in a family of 6, what is the ratio
of care to distance
knowledge to silence

the longer you follow the pattern
the closer you get

to the secrets
nested in secrets

lies nested in lies
nested in lies

ii. The golden ratio

$$\phi = 1 + \cfrac{1}{1 + \cfrac{1}{1 + \cfrac{1}{1 + \cfrac{1}{1 + \cfrac{1}{1 + \cdots}}}}}$$

look at the continued fraction
for phi, the golden ratio

all those ones
ones upon ones

ones to infinity
each one of us

a product of him
he wanted to see in us

his imagined perfection
his likely imagined genius IQ

that day in the kitchen he lined us up
cupped our foreheads

one by one
explained that this inherited curve

denoted a first-rate intellect
no room for fallibility, failure

none for the ordinary
defects of flesh and blood

which did not reflect him
so great his need to be golden

he'd have us silvered
like mirrors

iii. Infinity

one way to formulate
the irrational

capture
what the mind can't grasp

is to find the pattern that fits
and follow it

at a certain point
mark three small dots

which means:
go on to infinity

⋅ ⋅ ⋅

what the mind can't grasp
the body remembers

the patterns memory lays down
accrete, reveal themselves

as irrational fears
inexplicable aversions

the body so persistent
in its associations

leaping at a sound
the real-time brain has already recognised

like the lag of thunder
post lightning flash

as though the sound has travelled
back in time

to set off the old alarm
the house you grew up in

may have been sold
twenty times over

the room where your small bed stood
may now hold a 75-inch TV

or a snooker table
or have been demolished

but still you cannot convince
the child you were

that the person entering the darkened bedroom
is your wife

Note: this poem was commissioned as a collaboration with mathematician Marty Ross (who supplied the maths), and appeared in *Cordite Poetry Review*.

The Far East | ADAM AITKEN

I remember the school ground:
eager to kill, I punched him, but gently, diplomatically,
orientally.

Why didn't I just
poison his sandwich?
Named the Inscrutable I was angrier and more silent
than I looked.

In private moments I would
devise sermons on fear and fathers

in the voice of my mother.

Having never given up
loving you, you became
the template of my becoming.

After so much talking,
so much cutting down of forests
to make the barricade

my mother just made more talk,
gesticulating to the Danish envoy
who, beaten down by humidity,
would never enjoy chillies.

But in the long run
I came to accept that
the Celtic poet in *Game of Thrones*
was hired to cut off foreign heads.

I share no need to fly to distant prisons
where a thug I could have been
stews on what it is that got him there.

Some days I'm so extreme,
in the sense of far away,
too far away to calculate a trade,
like Marco Polo locked in a castle
on the edges of a distant green sea.

But on a sliding scale I'm
neither Oriental nor mean.
My tender presence brings you the key:
the gates open, at least an inch,
and the corridor sounds again,
with all the merchants of my desire
wanting a sale, offering closure.

First Reading | ANDY KISSANE

We begin rehearsals in a freezing warehouse
that was once a factory reverberating with the hum
and clanking of shuttle looms and the numbing
routine of days that chilled down into the soul,
that accumulated a tally of impoverished hours
spent tending a thread, a line of cotton, a line
of wool, all spooling and unspooling without end.
How privileged I am to be working at what I love,
to be collaborating with four men and five women
on a project that is destined for applause. I am
not one for speeches and group improvisations.
I will not impose some predetermined method
on the material. Instead, we sit around the table
and read the play. The lilt, grain and timbre
of their voices fills the room. There is no showing off,
no competition, simply the pleasure of imagining it
all unfold, as if a parachute is spread between us
ready to catch whatever shines and bounce it past our faces
while we watch it wobble, ricochet and spin. There is
not much to do but immerse myself in the listening.
And when Thao leaves her daughter, Mai, to go south
during the war, I suddenly see my father standing
next to my mother on the steps of the Saigon Opera House,
I see him buying a lottery ticket from a man with an open
suitcase and sitting down at a wedding feast with his friends—
all these young men smiling over bowls of rice. I must admit
that I'm hoping to find my father, or the ghost of my father,
that I long to be lifted up and swung through the air again,
to be wrapped up in his arms, to feel his cheek pressing
against mine, not the way he used to greet me, but now,
in this warehouse, in the pulse of this reading, to have
and hold more than the day when we last saw him,
when along with his ARVN comrades he shed
his uniform and abandoned his army boots,
leaving them unlaced and empty on a once frantic street.

Flannel Flowers | OMAR MUSA

Called forth from the scorched earth, these flannel flowers bloom
once every fifty years; grey-pink umbrellas, tiny, feathered, furred like
moth wing, constellated across this burnt out canyon; we trek through
blackened banksias, lignotubers gnarled and twined in the peat, their burst pods
like so many eyes and mouths, omnidirectional cameras, pointed every which
way: *out*, over the valley where the cliffs beyond are divided as if by design,
upright planes down which pewter streams when it rains, sometimes; *up*, at the
bluest, memoryless sky; *and towards us*, lunching in a hollow in the rock.
Miri is crouching down with Kimi to look at the flannel flowers in the dust,
and the purple fringe lilies amongst them, which are delicate beyond belief
and last only for one day. Miri is not to know that this might be the only time
she (or we) will ever see these blooms, inherit through touch their grace, touch
them as if testing a new word—Miri is two years old and her world yet ahead.
The old couple who arrive as we leave have come to sight them for the first and
last time, like certain eclipses, like comets, these heavenly bodies   at our feet.
Last week, Jesse saw a woman shake ashes from the cliffs here, out into the canyon,
where the winds whistle and sing hymns beneath black cockatoos' wings, that
riffle the bracts and bow the heads of flannel flowers, who lay so long in refuge,
made possible only by the perfect conspiracy of catastrophic fire, time, and deluge.

FOR GIORGIO | KEN BOLTON

from some lines of Tony Towle's

Hang it all, Giorgio de Chirico,
there is only the one battered faucet—
pouring out the ongoing present, in the minutes we possess.
Unstoppable. There is *no* rest.
Whether you live in Rome or Port Elliot,

there is none. Better than living in Dorset. All three tho
bring, to my mind, calm. Rome's traffic,
necessarily, *compels you to seek it*—a darkened room, a quiet square. Port
     Elliot suggests a certain
melancholy—but restful. And Dorset? a boarding house, a curtain
pulled against the drear sea view, the esplanade malefic—

& *empty*: dour sea wall, where lamp posts, regularly spaced,
make their unconvincing case for the decorative;
the sea itself—& the sky, just barely differentiated
from the water beneath. Time, here, is exterminated, greyed,
denied purpose. One would turn inside to a television—if

in Dorset. Let us not—in any sense of the term—
go there (*& in fact I've never been*, nor you,
Giorgio). We confine ourselves to Rome—
& Port Elliot, with its fine beach. In the town's South Seas bookshop a tome
devoted to your work sits, has sat for a year or more—for you

to purchase, or to rummage thru—looking for the good ones.
Ha, ha, ha. My joke. They're *all* good
one way or another. I've been thru it many times, as must have others.
(It continues to look … '*fresh*'. 'Ish'.) The loopy ones I sort of covet …
But I have a lot at home—many a book

with works by *you*, Giorgio. My most enduring

enthusiasm. You set me on the road to loving paintings.

You, & one or two others, whom I've forgotten. ('Relegated'.)

(Nolde, Ensor.) *Then* how did it go? Munch; the contemplative

yet intense Cezanne; Matisse & Picasso—their unremitting

& inventive purpose; the great of the past—Rembrandt, Velazquesz, Piero,

Raphael & Titian. The Baroque, the Rococo. My hero

Manet, & so on …   Pollock. And

—who have I left out?—Kirchner, Beckmann,

 … (Rauschenberg). The *minor* greats—Marquet, Filippo

de Pisis. And, 'Now', … Oehlen, Christopher Wool. Time

never stands still. The faucet again. Where the element plunges out

in terrifying chunks, heavy with implication—*of your making*.

Timeless & urgent. I could *stand* beside that faucet—

lounge—metaphysical, yes—like the guy in the drawing, *The Mysterious Baths.*

Don't make me revisit Dorset—Bournemouth, Weymouth—I couldn't.

ASIEL ADÁN SÁNCHEZ

: On September 26, 2014, forty-three students disappeared from my mother's hometown of Iguala, Guerrero.
: The group left in two stolen Estrella de Oro buses from the Normalist Rural School Isidro Burgos in Ayotzinapa towards the township of Iguala.
: Fifteen years earlier, my mother and I, standing at the same bus stop with two economy tickets in our hands.
: Witness accounts state
: Students in Rural Normalist Schools are taught to till the soil, harvest maize,
: Among other Marxist-Leninist practices.
: *Ay, policía, qué lástima me das: teniendo tú las armas ¡no puedes protestar!*
: In government reports, the evidence is laid out neatly
: One-hundred and ninety-five shells at the crime scene;
: Seventy-seven 7.62x39-caliber from AK-47s;
: Eighty-six .223-caliber from HK G36s, Berettas and Bushmasters;
: Eighteen 7.62x51-caliber from G3s;
: Seven 9mm;
: Six .380-caliber;
: One .22-caliber;
: Six bodies;

: Three students.
: *Mijo, he looks like you.*
: Witness accounts state
: Two were killed by gunshots.
: One was found the following day.
: His face had been partly flayed.
: Let me be clear, what we share today are only updates of the investigation underway.
: They are not, nor do they claim to be, final conclusions.
: Still, my aunt refuses to open the door for anybody.
: In press conferences, the government produced over 100 witness statements and fragments of evidence.
: None can explain the presence of the federal army.
: *They were, they said there were 44, I heard- but I didn't count them one by one, no. They came in a big truck.*
: Could you say it again?
: *With diesel and gasoline, we bathed the bodies with diesel and gasoline.*
: Witness accounts state
: The students were unarmed.
: They were last seen being escorted into police cars and army vehicles.

: *Porque vivos se los llevaron, vivos los queremos.*

: As stated by Attorney General Jesús Murillo Karam,

: The investigation allows us to conclude without a doubt that the students were killed, incinerated and thrown into the San Juan river.

: When I ask my mother, she tells me she doesn't remember where San Juan is.

: It was the narcos, *mjio*, come eat.

: When you were little, there was a place near the highway we used to go every Sunday.

: Chicken and rabbit stew; the best pozole you could get.

: To this day, the remains have not been found.

: In summer, we used to swim at the Laguna de Tuxpan.

: The cool waters, the knowing hills.

Free Sonnet* | JOSIE JOCELYN SUZANNE

For Em

The pride of heavy rings, the pomp of glamour
glinting—the art of your unnatural charms;
gardenias in corsage, arranging winters
die from dissolving—caresses in your arms.
Your mouth—gossamer with glass engravings—
translates the glass of verse perfectly.
Beneath satin curtains, knowing—billowing
open—your breast bursts in pale luxuries.
The sapphire's reflection darkens your blue eyes;
the uncertain whirlpool of your roiling body
traces a wake of gold in the waters of light.
When you pass, guarding a private smile
—gold pastel, laden with perfume and finery—
I dream of your body's splendour, free, naked.

Speak to me, in your voice like running water
when the breath of confessions is given
up at last. Speak to me—if you're so driven—in words
cruel and mocking, but shelter me in your heady
chants. In this veiled tone that charms and
intoxicates me, when my caress goes astray
in your tangling hair, express your hopes, regrets and
desires, O my lover, full of harmony
and music. I will listen to your voice and delicate
song. I will no longer seek to understand, I will
listen, seeking—if not total oblivion—rest
at least. Because, if you stop, if only a single
moment I would hear… I would hear in the depths
of the silence, something awful, crying terribly.

* Translation from the French, original by Renée Vivienne, from her collection *Etudes et Préludes*, from Lemarre Publishing house, 1909, republished by ErosOnyx 2007, via the university of Michigan.

Garden Dreaming | KIM CHENG BOEY

Almost full moon, the night sprinkled with stars, salt grains
sown over the obsidian bowl of the southern sky
and I am again bewildered by the bountiful
beauty of the orange and lemon trees
in our backyard, each spring an unfailing flush
of rich sweet blossoms, bee-haunted in the day
but ghostly silent in the moonlight flooding
the garden and house.

A man can get scent-drunk on such
riches, on the heady bouquet the trees
wear, the fragrant nimbus around their crowns,
and on the perfumed starlight sifting
through the screen of harp-like branches to kiss
the dew rising from the glistening skin
of transfigured grass. The house breathes this in
so deeply it floats free of time's shadows,
the questions of home forgotten.

Fifteen years cultivating this plot
of earth, battling the weeds and drought,
the aftermath of hail and storms that stripped
the trees almost bare, the rounds of feeding
this earth, the orange, the plum and peach trees,
of watching the perennials rise from winter
sleep like reminders.
Surely these years of planting and growing
will go into the mind's compost heap;
days of digging, of rousing odours
locked in the soil, watering the garden
with dreams of belonging, of shovel-feeding
the plants with the mix made up of memories
of the living and the dead, days when I forgot
about writing and where we come from

in the spade's honest bite of dirt, in its scoop
of loosened soil, in laying out stanzaic plots
of basil and rosemary, lavender and thyme, the need
for words forgotten in the calendar of turning
leaves, the sap of pruned branches and freshly mown grass.

Time now to say goodbye to our trees,
to the potted herbs, to the resurgent jonquils and daffodils,
to the low-slung Southern Cross and the deep drift
of these native stars. To the pale blue gum leaning
from the neighbour's yard, and countless ranks of eucalypts
beyond the street, where the bush begins, miles of trees
whose names will whisper-haunt our lives.

Soon summer will dazzle
our trees with orange and lemon fruit,
and the currawong, the magpie and honeyeaters
will plunder the fig and peach. As the days
lengthen the cicada choir will strike up and will not cease
till it expends its soul and becomes spent shells
on the trees and house.

Soon we will be far from the garden, and the questions
of home will awaken in our gardenless state,
vex us like weeds in a different latitude
under a muffled sky,
and this starlight sprinkled among citrus blossoms
will call with the shiver of distance in the screen of close
branches like so many roads between stars,
with the scent of memory, the echoes of home.

Gunny Sack Rebellion | ELENA GOMEZ

I'll fit you in my little gunny sack here,
You can jump right in, I'm a golden fibre,
A vegetable text, you study it at school or
wrap this shit up with it. Christian calls us

There's an act for the rugs, but by many arms.
Begin a space of jute:
I'm comatose at the factory entrance
  the fibre stings back

Before the civil disobedience act
    workers hands
        muscles, tendons, ligaments,
   porous prints, cultural citizens:
    out of here: the planetary moment
Taken, the hourly rate, collected, disesteemed, my flailing marker of extraction
& meanwhile, we obey Notley: to 'maintain a state of disobedience', or
        inversions, the gathered
tools of Progress—of a hellish internment—right there, we said, you said:

Look Away & thereafter
  I'm your Golden Yarn

1928: a first general strike, see, at *Ludlow Jute Mill*

For the other bodies, the laundry basket, cushion hold
  —I refuse melodic increments

But we're chromatic in the afterlife
fibrous dust, shipped
   sacks

Demand soared, we saved the gunny
bags, rescued certain products

a Refusal in the Notleyean
sense, and the Civil

The Heart of the Advocate | ANGELA COSTI

'One word can change a truth into a lie.'

With some help, she was able to turn her story into an affidavit. However, the story is fighting to escape the format of the form. The sequencing of events needs to focus on dates and times. Each and every word uttered, gesture made, sound heard, visual cue should be documented as if it were an inventory. What did he say to her, how did he put his body into hers, when did she say No, how did she say No, did she say No, how long for? His Word. Her Word. His Body. Her Body. Their Body. No Body. No. Yes. No. And *if* he did, what were *her* motives?

'One doubt can change a truth into a lie.'

She is 31 years old. Her middle name is Haralampo, which is her father's first name. She wanted to be a lawyer before she became an Assistant Manager at IGA. It wasn't her manager. It wasn't her boyfriend. She was a professional soccer player eight years ago. Her father coached her. She kept a diary. She set her diary free in a fire, when she left home. Her older sister is not talking to the family and lives somewhere in Sydney. Her mother is beginning to forget the ingredients for spanakopita. Her middle name is Haralampo, which is her father's first name.

'Justice must not be confused with law.'

When the story first arrived in my office, it was pent up with years of outrage and guilt. It was the feral cat, the wild horse, the charred koala. Taming, containing, coaxing the story towards the malignant law is difficult when the client is clinging to hope. And it's painful when my heart whimpers with the strain of upholding a library of outdated words.

The story is now confined to the form. The document lies passively on my desk as I reach over with my pen. This pen will have her sign the document imprisoning her truth. But there's a problem. She is sitting across from me, daring me to look into her eyes. Not picking up the pen.

'Betrayal is harder to compensate than rape.'

Hummingbird Country | DEBBIE LIM

My aunt says never trust a hummingbird. Never trust
    a creature which flies backwards with ease, whose feet
were made useless for walking. My aunt is not a real
       aunt but a cat shaped like a woman. She runs her claws

across the ceiling and drags my heart from room to room
    in a grey ribbed mouth. She stalks in gardens. Steals all
the hummingbird feeders. Later I hear their glass bones
      jittering apart in the sack when she kisses them

with a hammer. My aunt says never trust an animal
    that is armless like god—in each eye sits a minute camera.
She gouges out each flowering bush by the house,
      installs heavy velvet blackout curtains.

Bad days she binds me to the chair. I practice violet
    palpitations and miniature thoughts, teach my fingers
to flutter so fast you can't see them. I wear skin brooches:
      tender blues, green. She hasn't noticed I am mastering

the art of iridescence. Evenings I collect slugs and grind them
    to a paste. Gather lichens, compare the tensile
strength of different kinds of spiders' silk. In my head I hone
      a delegation of moons. My tongue lengthens

and grooves. Under darkness I rehearse the languages
    they will speak in the new country: Snowcap, Emerald,
Hermit, Bee … When she comes in at night to check my breath,
      I sink deep into torpor. I am learning to sleep

like the dead in a thimble of moss. Each morning on waking
    I perform fresh wingbeats in bed. Marvel at how
small I've become. Tomorrow break of day, I will be
       glint of raindrop. Genuflection of light. Rotation of air—

afterwards she will lift back the sheet and find nothing
    but a tiny pair of dropped arms.

Note: This poem draws on a line from Norman Dubie's poem 'Hummingbirds': 'They will be without arms like god.' Snowcap, Emerald, Hermit and Bee are varieties of hummingbirds.

I have become psychologically linked to a humpback whale
| CLAIRE ALBRECHT

I don't know how it happened but I woke one morning tethered
across oceans, over landmass to a very large brain
approximately 4.6 kilograms—not as big as I thought it'd be
but it might have lost something in the transmission

the hook in my own head tugs as I go about my daily things
and the direction slowly moves like an orbit
the whale as he follows his trail north with the shorebirds
is a comet, an explorer before boundaries, while I wash towels

and I don't know enough about string theory to explain how
we might have been pulled together in this manner
or about quantum physics at all, come to think of it
but I know his big whale brain holds 'spindle neurons' just like mine

I imagine these as little blonde girls spinning straw into thoughts
really they are just root systems of neurons that teach us to love
and cry and talk to each other, and it seems beautiful to me
that the whale carries these too, like a songbook

in the night my 1.5kg brain writes poems with him
and we move together beneath the surface of conscious thought
I find myself waking sometimes by the sea, in wet socks
and I wonder if he sleep-swims to the shore like this

by coincidence or design we are the same age
(I can't tell you how I know this, but I do)
the same anxieties swim through our nervous systems
and along the thin silvery cord that connects us

our huge dark eyes stare into the same murky distance
we are afraid of the darkness ahead, but we move always
helped along by the comfort pulled from each other
we're strangers between realms, remote in our seas

I try to talk to him directly, forcing the connection to grow
invite him to daiquiris at the swim-up bar
but I don't know where he is exactly and I don't want him
to end up beached. that is our biggest fear

and it hovers over us daily, a dry eye crusting on sand
stranded, restless, while our body lies paralysed and useless
there is nothing satisfying about rest
we are always rolling the spindle, waving our fins in the air

I don't know why the whale pulls me along
I really don't. all I know is that I am not the frozen head
of an explorer in the Antarctic. not severed, but strung taut
and the instrument of the earth is vibrating

I want/don't want a place | A FRANCES JOHNSON

I want a place
past poisoned soils where
moony cattle stare and low,
asking patient why.
But abattoirs dissemble, cool
metallic grins hidden behind
slaughtered hills, shower-
capped workers falling out
at 4pm, blanked by blood,
grim mesentery tangles,
a record day's offal weight.

I want no zoos, no brittle
arcadias, rewilded bridges
spanning eight-lane freeways,
birthmarked by old roadkill.
Close underfunded ecology
centres, cheerful Alice pushing
forms and crying *Sign, Give, Leave us
a message. Please! Please!*

I want no old-growth flyover,
concealed battery shadow:
hens, coal, uranium, light, heat—
time leaking and degrading,
guarded sites that mine and mine
and still say 'mine', all mine.

Let the aggrieved 'I' cede
to hummed insect edicts,
silent fish councils, weary
roars of trash-loving bears,
the understorey's riotous
demand for fire. Retire 'I';

let it hang its head
and not conspire with
mea culpa's last egotism:
lazy planetary leave-taking.

De-bunk moss-dreamed no-place,
caretaking outsourced, poorly paid.
Let thronged 'us' walk shadow places
that tell tales of toxic time and make time
full again, ask more than patient why.

Landscapes, with Poem | MARJAN MOSSAMMAPARAST

i.

The first vision: it was prehistoric,
the gargantuan ferns reflected in what he called
a *billabong*. We didn't know what it heralded,
wider than the promise of platypus
the arresting half-risen stumps of drowned giants,
when on we gingerly picked through mud
in our ill-prepared shoes
      I had wanted to visit the lake for years
for years I had been alone, on the misty drive to Forrest
had braved the unsealed road only once
and then only halfway, afraid of being a girl   *Where is Yugoslavia?*
without reception, and all that   *Past the curatorial intent.*
forest
      It can dwarf you.
The light hardly reached. The rainbow horizon
had closed in, where we had wound up from the breakers,
the unrelenting open-mouthed dominion of surf
into which we could

Always be afraid. Awe
that is what lives on this continent, not small things:
the footprint of a megasaur, among whose reeds
      a duck.

ii.

Echuca: the barges are busy with incantation.
The word *spiritual* drops from the mouth of a woman
for the first time, into the river.

It sinks, upon this scratchy red-gum churning course
with its load of goods, with memory   *Where are the bags of flour?*
of its load, of goods, when Bush was Frontier.   *Past the curatorial intent.*
Spirit is the frontier. I am not Australian.

iii.

A windowpane of light above the descent of evening
I know there is memory in that, grasped in the outline of trees,
the white peaks of waves in the distance beyond the pier
in echoes I must now explain in words, for poems
stuck to windowpanes, where Christos left a tiny shark
hanging from the hook of his fishery, the globe of its right eye
a dead glass encased in gelatine. Here is the poem,
this self-reflexive patterning. He was ousted by the market
driven past the day's catch, and we—readers of line-work, augurs
who stopped for those taped-up faded handwritten
notes of ascent   *Where is it written?*
stop now for our reflection. It shows us *real life*   *Past the curatorial intent.*
the strain of offices, coffee, catastrophe in the mouth.
Down by the swing bridge, the estuary cuts, cuts the sand
continually rewriting the moon.

iv.

"If one no longer has land but has the memory of land
then one can make a map"

All this whiteness makes me cry.
I seek succour in a Vietnamese fabric store,

that conjures a land adjacent to another adjacency   *In the dot and the line*
and so on, riding a carpet that might take me closer   *that say to me, Nothing.*
to the places adjacent to my dreaming.
In Magic Dollar I say to the woman, You have everything
东西, that lie between East and West.
Her door is interval, sluice gate, through which my heart
predates concepts, nicely rounded out.
Somewhere مرجان is the name of a girl
mounted on a plinth. I am waiting, like the stolen,
for a handful of earth in my coat.

Notes:

东西 = dōngxī (thing), composed of the Chinese characters for East (东, dōng) and West (西, xī)

مرجان = Marjon/Marjan (Farsi)

Section iv epigraph is a quote from an unnamed source at the Jewish Museum of Australia, St Kilda.

Last appointment of the day | KIRWAN HENRY

We already knew you were gone
before we got to the clinic.
Our appointment was the last of the day.
The lady did not see us waiting.
She walked by wearing her designs on the afternoon.
"…have to tell them about a miscarriage"
was thrown to a colleague over her shoulder.
She said it like babies were bottles of water
or cups of tea. I did not tell her
we had already done our shopping for the week.
Instead I pretended I hadn't heard.
She must have realised too late
that our ears were in range
and well and truly shot.
Still, I worried about what she thought of me.

Your father worried too. When we got home
he proposed helpful phone calls and a weekend away.
I buried the forms and pamphlets the lady gave me
in the bottom drawer where I keep my scarves.
I do not wear them. I do not feel pretty. I am an open sore.
I cry on and off like in books and songs.
Your father holds me close as if I am overflowing.

Every morning I take a form out of the drawer
and offer my insides to a nurse
who reminds of my aunty.
We discuss the fineness of my veins.
When I get home I keep busy.
The lady from the clinic interrupts my lunch
to let me know how little of you is left. I thank her
and tear up all but one of the pamphlets
she pressed upon me. The one I keep I file under
'Miscellaneous'. It does not belong under
'Receipts and Warranties'.
I cannot say "Fix this"
and I do not want a new one.

last swim before space flight | RORY GREEN

you'll just swap one form of floating for another
they said, you're still weightless. do they know
how heavy the ocean feels? how the harvest
moon can sow a net of light, billowing, aureate,
ensnare a season before it can even arrive.
how space smells rotten and sulfuric
nothing like the briny sweetness of a coastal swell,
the way it wraps around and dizzies you,
pulls you magnetic to its rumbling source. do
they not know the moon's shimmer of spume over water
is a mere echo, a soft tug on something more unknowable
and forgiving than the limping void of space?
how can they ignore the protozoic shell whispers
of ancestors who found this rock and chose to stay,
what it means to be a reservoir of care here.
how it feels to be joined to this vital, amniotic thing, to
wallow as every perfect earthly being has before you.
you know what they don't—that the weight of it
is the point, how it feels like launching
without ever leaving the ground.

The Last Male White Rhinoceros | NANDI CHINNA

This morning slowly
chewing on my oats and milk
I listen to the radio news bulletin,
gaze through the window at the brown birds splashing in the birdbath
the last male white Rhinoceros
died in captivity today.

Then I'm under the shower
water rolling into and out of
my eyes, with a ghost,
or a joker, or a friend
the last male white rhinoceros
stares at me with a sad accusing eye.

At the first meeting of the day
the last male white rhinoceros sits in
on the discussion—agenda—
museum collections,
ephemera, banners, stickers,
human-sized papier-mâché turtles
giant cockatoo puppets
and a threadbare sweat stained blue T-shirt
 declaring *Save the Wetlands.*
The last male white rhinoceros
swallows a sarcastic snort,

Well?

The museum photographer asks us to pose
at the edge of a lake with black swans

in the background, *good, good, now turn*
and look, can you see that smudged white blur
lumbering out of the frame? The last male
white rhinoceros would have loved it here.

Later at the shops I consult my mental
list—*milk, cheese, tea, ginger, garlic,*
the last male white rhinoceros died this morning,
his name was Sudan, he was 45 years old.

Back in the office a mountain
of e-mails, requests, dates, meetings
Dear, thank you, best wishes to the great
white male rhinoceros, the last of his kind
turns his back on me: no reflection
no shadow, no desire, no appetite,
no offspring, no habitat. Loneliness
fills the room, the house, the street,
the empty, hot, burning sky.

Over dinner I turn on the TV
grazing through my salad
there is no mention of the last
male white rhinoceros on the 6.30 news,
just a rhinoceros-like shape dissolving
into pixels as I press the OFF button.

At the evening meeting two town planners,
fidget in their hot grey suits.
They refer to their powerpoint presentation,

demographics of a burgeoning suburb,
19,000 people in the area, expected to grow
to 38,000 in the next five to ten years.
The last male white rhinoceros hovers restlessly
at the back of the room, hooves clicking
on the polished boards.

The question is—
where will people play?
Not enough playing fields
allocated to the housing development,
city council predicts the need
for more sporting facilities.
The floorboards creak, heads turn
as a greyish white rump disappears
through the automatic sliding doors.

My bicycle hisses through the wide
suburban street, I pedal on
past my house, keep going
legs pumping harder up the hill
past remnant bush rustling, soughing,
feathers, leaves, turning, rattling, bile rising
in my mouth I push the pedals
the last male white rhinoceros keeping up
the pace as I heel into corners, sprint
the flats, huff up inclines past houses

with doors left open to let out heat,
humans laughing at televisions as the night
seeps into the room and the last male
white rhinoceros lingers outside I hurl
the bike back downhill where the last
male white rhinoceros is waiting to greet me,
an excruciating grief teeming with flies
and ants, his flesh leaving now as we lie
down to sleep. *Don't forget this day, never
forget* he whispers to me as we curl
into the mattress, spooning the quiver
of each other's sentience.

In the morning the weather has broken,
eight months of blue are covered by cloud,
small brown birds bounce from bush
to birdbath, I step outside to find
the last male white rhinoceros has gone.

Leafless–Leafs | LOUISE CRISP
(East Gippsland foothill forest: Gunaikurnai country)

Words are leafless

In the forest some words are too loud

Most words belong to someone else

The sheen of words precludes listening

Leafs wait to be heard

Felled: the story between earth and sky

Trees are determined as the rocks

The middle story

Is dialogue? Logging

The tracks of words eviscerate echidnas

Leafs align along a ridge

Do all the words inculcate colonialism?

Greater gliders cannot eat your words however leafy

The colonisers' word morphs into enforcement

The route into the valley is not shown by words

Forest: a word with many leafs

Words that are seen, leafs that are not

The track vanishes off the map but the route remains

Leafs as necessary as touch

The old forest…

The creek is not leafless, words float on the surface

Live from Gaza | SARA M SALEH

funeral these headlines
        their insidious &
        the facts
        the theatricality of chaos
our lands
our traumas
        right to self defence
        until 'complete quiet'
yesterday &
today &
tomorrow

report the stories of
        siren
        shelter
        monster
        mayhem
            &
        death toll
the bias of those
under bombardment
        the false equivalence
        the certainty
in script
    &
circumstance
in distortion
        in the twitch and spasm
        the absolute ~~lie~~ loss
telling
the truth
   &
power
of
        the narrative
the may/be in the testimony
the complicated in the detail
the question in alleged
the myth in question

existence

                            is
                         assault
                            is
                       escalation
                            is
                        conflict
                            is
                    dozens killed
                            is
                      air strikes

investigation

                            is
                       children
                            is
                         shield
                            is
                    the militants
                            is
                       schools
                            is
                         sides

Gaza

                            is
                       retaliation
                            is
                    the buildings
                            is
               humanitarian crisis
                            is
                          strip
                            is
                       ceasefire

freedom

                                          is
                                     sand
                                        is
                                   world
                                      is
                                   cage
                                      is
                                 murder
                                      is
                                   ours

existence is

                                                          assault is
                                                     escalation is
                                                        conflict is
                                             dozens killed is
                                                    airstrike is
                                             investigation is
                                                   children is
                                                      shield is
                                            the militants is
                                                 schools is
                                                     sides is
                                                    Gaza is
                                             retaliation
                                        the buildings is
                             humanitarian crisis is
                                                  strip is
                                             ceasefire is
                                           freedom is
                                               sand is
                                               world is
                                                cage is
                                           murder is
                                             ours is

In memory of

In memory of Baraa al-Gharabli
In memory of Mustafa Obaid
In memory of Yazan al-Masri
In memory of Marwan al-Masri
In memory of Rahaf al-Masri
In memory of Ibrahim al-Masri
In memory of Hamada al-Emour
In memory of Ammar al-Emour
In memory of Mahmoud Tolbeh
In memory of Yahya Khalifa
In memory of Fawziya Abu Faris
In memory of Muhammad-Zain al-Attar
In memory of Amira al-Attar
In memory of Islam al-Attar
In memory of Suheib al-Hadidi
In memory of Yahya al-Hadidi
In memory of Osama al-Hadidi
In memory of Abdurrahman al-Hadidi
In memory of Yara al-Qawlaq
In memory of Hala al-Qawlaq
In memory of Rula al-Qawlaq
In memory of Zaid al-Qawlaq
In memory of Qusai al-Qawlaq
In memory of Adam al-Qawlaq
In memory of Ahmad al-Qawlaq
In memory of Hana al-Qawlaq
In memory of Dima al-Ifranji
In memory of Yazan al-Ifranji
In memory of Mira al-Ifranji
In memory of Amir al-Ifranji
In memory of Dana Ishkontana
In memory of Lana Ishkontana
In memory of Yahya Ishkontana
In memory of Zain Ishkontana
In memory of Tala Abu Elouf
In memory of Tawfiq Abu Elouf
In memory of Rafeef Abu Dayer
In memory of Dima Asaliyah
In memory of
In memory of
In memory of
In memory of
In memory o
In memory
In memor
In memo
In mem
In me
In m
In

I

Notes:
The last section of this poem inspired by M. NourbeSe Philip's Zong! #24.
The names of children killed in Israel's attack on Gaza in May 2021 is not an exhaustive list. There were dozens more Palestinians, including children.
This poem was first published in *Rabbit Poetry Journal*'s issue: *Reportage*.

Losing Alexandria | LENI SHILTON

for Maya Cifali born 1937

In your desert garden a bower bird mimics falling water,
the cat's bell.
We talk, and travel to places far from here,
through mosaic streets, past the bazaar.
We are in distant lands, and cities—
Egypt, Alexandria, Paris, Tehran, Canberra, finally, Alice Springs.

Memories lean one into another—
ceramic tiles, blue shards under your feet,
the spices of your mother's kitchen.
Voices rise from the marketplace where, as a child you ran
in the cumin-scented air.

A hundred years of your family fleeing Spain, Algeria or Italy
meet here on the western arm of the Nile
like two great waves looking for peace.

History folds as your father tells you—
Egypt is for the Egyptians now.
And you must leave Alexandria, the country of your birth.
You step from the wharf
tears and salt spray taking you away.
In Paris, studying among friends,
the terrible war done with—
we felt we were reorganising the world
the generation of children who survived—
and the sad growing truth that the work is never done.

The wide lake, the mountains of Switzerland
peaceful routine, work, studies, babies,
white wine, weekend with the family,
it could have remained the same forever, but it didn't.

Always the traveller, now with two daughters
long immigrant journeys to the dry sheep fields of Canberra.
The language expert in this dull city of one language.

Years later with your husband, an adventure to Iran,
where Tehran's snow-covered mountains glow in the dimming light,
and the wave of *Allah Akbar* rises up the hills, in a chilling rush.

To the far wet islands of Papua New Guinea
and the shock of dark at the days end.
The crash of bats in the palms, air pungent
as incessant bird call rings in your ears.

Then, one day you arrived in Alice Springs,
where the air is the air of Alexandria.

You find a stand of date palms regal in the heat, and know
you can finally unpack your books—
French and Arabic next to the languages of the desert.

Here you dance with your Aboriginal sisters—your teachers.
They call you by a new name *Nakamarra*,
hold you between their bodies
and dance, as the rhythm of the land rolls through them.
They teach you stories of this desert so far from the desert of your birth.

All my life, I have been looking for where I belong,
I know now my home is here in this desert,
here in this yard with the bower bird, the bottle brush, the gum tree.

Mandala | BONNY CASSIDY

The house is small, only a cottage, and sits picking at its dread.

I don't want to write about this house, I must let it out of the poem

like smoke carrying down the misty river, around the bend of leaning trunks away.

*

I want to write about Erica McGilchrist.

We share a birthday
ruled in the tarot by THE STAR

water into water
water into earth
water into air

*

I found it hideous, her early 1950s expressionism—
angular anguished women, just clowns without Joy Hester's humour.

Others went to war to find these extinguished eyes, Erica went to Kew.
By 1955 the number of female patients at Kew Mental Hospital was 464, roughly equal to that of male, although Erica said they were 'perhaps thousands'. Unlike Albert Tucker she didn't go to gawp at primitive states, she taught troubled people to paint. The anxious patients preferred to simply colour the linear designs that Erica drew and drew.

And so, I change my mind about her women behind fences or in mirrors. They aren't insane. They feel sad because their babies died

or they lost a midnight argument with themselves
nose to nose. You can go mad by being told you are.

After her hospital classes, Erica drew pastels of women driving wheelchairs and
toy cars.

*

It was a couple of days before the anniversary of Erica's death
that I first saw her work. In the Reeds' cottage at Heide, under the men on its
mantles, her flags are brighter stars.

Within months of Kew, the pictures by the art therapist were updated
by dry-fucking-cleanable paintings! Done on the floor using acrylics on linen
they look like kitsch tea-towels. A heraldry

of x-ray animals and hatching nicked from desert artists
and Mountford's Arnhem Land collection. Helmeted, cassocked figures and
crowds of masks.

> 'The purpose of a wall hanging is less serious [than a painting]. It should
> be decorative, a backdrop to the life that goes on around it.'

Maybe Erica purged something—the Modernist—
because later she regretted these backdrops for Melbourne sitting rooms.

*

Ambiguous objects
geometric dropping
into patterns like Te
tris

intricate
eschers of houndsteeth
chainlinked, riddles of scaffolding
and chevroned drains to the half-
closed eye a cyborg garden, teratoma.

*

Sometimes she arrived after history, often she arrived before it.

*

Sidney Nolan was reducing emblems while Erica watched them form: pigment in a jar of water. Crystals join seamlessly.

Fractures. Refractions. These recur and act like loopholes letting her through into the next phase. But they hang together, they don't splinter apart.

Symmetry: what repeats
Enigma: what resists
Emblem: what gains meaning.

*

Working in Munich in the early sixties freed her
line from shape

and woke up what she deeply knew—
that human cruelty lives next door

fills
the standard
veins
of a subway map.

Returning home, she was to realise
'A profound sense of the vulnerability of old and new Australians.'

*

She mightn't have approved of the tarot with its archetypes.
She sought pattern for infinite variety.
She got into knots but avoided ties.

Lucy Lippard diagnosed 'female imagery' in Erica's work; 'dripping with it,' the American said. This was a philosophical puzzle that Erica could not solve. Was a sexed bank of imagery reductive, or another escape from the cultural patterns she was coming to loathe?

> 'The recipe in 1972 was: an Australian landscape with maybe an Aboriginal figure or two (as decoration only—woe betide any artist who introduced social comment of any kind), the whole to be painted in "Drysdale" colours—reds, oranges and brown, or alternatively the colour scheme could be based on turquoise blue.'

Under her star, Erica was making mandalas; thick with pale glazes, they refuse representation and they bleed for loss. Forms of grief and re-enchantment, a cosmic design

*

Art sickens, art heals.

The day after first seeing Erica's work, I hear that Kate Jennings has died.

The first time I read *Mother, I'm Rooted* I was an undergraduate and found a copy at Alan Wearne's suggestion.

The second time, I was a postgraduate understanding how a second wave feminist poetics could surround so much work but not include all of it.

I'd understood the theoretical problem of white feminism but now I felt the impossibility of 'shoulder to shoulder.' The third time I read the collection, I was designing a new feminist poetry anthology with Jessica L Wilkinson. We admired Jennings' open call-out to contributors—an approach we would homage—but there was no way that our book could repeat its untroubled sense of collective representation.

Erica had already found another way. Inspired by American feminist organising, in 1975 she co-founded the Women's Art Register, calling out nationally for female artists to submit slides of their work. It grows. Any

female-identifying, non-binary or trans artist can join the Register with a
membership payment. They are held in a living archive of practice.

*

I find Erica's work again, later, this time breathing in a white cube
between neon strips and slogans, the hard edges that her soft craft knows.

Installed by contemporary female collaborators alongside their own
as though it were yesterday and she's slipped out of the gallery for a kebab.

This is when (I'm beginning to walk)
she flowers into embroidery. Movable
but not decoration, this time—in the eighties
she's threading some knowledge into the fern (heart) and necklace (uterus).
It's an optical code. What it knows, I mean, cannot be said in another way.

*

I pull the curtain aside and there's another behind: a tapestry of mist filling
the spaces between stringy trunk and new leaf.

A chunk of blue basalt sits on the deck like a sleeping animal, like the chough's
nest a clay trough balanced on a bough.

Its pits are sharp in my foreground, against the bush that floats up like a
waterfall.

Note: This poem was started and finished on unceded Eastern Kulin Nation lands, I pay respects to the elders of Wurundjeri (Heide) and Dja Dja Wurrung (Chewton). I thank the Women's Art Register for access to its archives on Erica McGilchrist.

Mandelbrot Set | JENNIFER HARRISON

A fractal mathematical world discovered in 1980 by Benoit Mandelbrot, as reported in Cosmos *17, 2008*

i

~ dots of colour   points on a complex
       number plane where the x horizontal axis
represents the 'real' part number
       and the vertical y gives us unseen
space   the imaginary i   x=iy
       and i2 =−1   which is
the infinite horizon's periphery
       of scolia   stellate forms   narrow sky
water   earth   data   an exiguous eternity...
       a free fractal generator
ChaosPro (www.chaospro.de)
       takes our most malleable maps
and gives back to us   neon lichen   estuaries
       snowflakes   black beetles   astral trees
tributaries   fjords   coastlines   budding
       spores and flowers   all the river mysteries
 Zeus might have seen from heaven
       or the shallop we imagined belonged to the gods
infinitely divine and wise...
       kaleidoscopic world   beautiful blaze
enlarged by looking   it took a man his entire life
       to decipher this hidden world
while Zeus had only immortality
       to juggle in the mountain's clouds
and olive trees   the blue ocean a scimitar
       leaning back on land's edge to gnaw
the fronds of fate   liturgies leave it up to our kind
       our eyes   to keep the smaller picture in mind ~

ii

~ a new set of chess pieces   unrecognised
  moves and checkmates   no single gene
or game clock to regulate strategy
  and the vertical y gives us unseen
space   the imaginary i   x=iy
  an elastic blueprint   each trait defined
by what we cannot see or hear or know
  an infant reaching for a mobile phone
listening for the sound of words   phrases
  sentences   imprisoned by lost languages...
ChaosPro (www.chaospro.de)...
  Alan Turing imagined a machine
that could decipher the arithmetical world
  without consciousness   calculation hurled
at the mind's handedness   cryptography
  (Daniel C. Dennett called Turing one of
the twigs on the 'Tree of Life' in the 2020 *New York*
  Review of Books)   his analytic
machines scything through intercepted Nazi
  codes with Darwinian practicality...
enlarged by looking   it took a man his entire life
  to decipher this hidden world
of spider webs   wasp nests   beaver dams...
  we have not met our lockdown grandchild
a face already loved beyond imagining
  heart-gesture inherited   transcending
space and time to un-net the spider   un-melt the ice
  un-dam the beaver   welcome to paradise ~

Marshmallow flowers | MITCHELL WELCH

This morning the veil the morning threw
the yawning dark was pale-flower white
and had my eyeballs in its breakfast milk.

Scrawled in chalk the morning walked
its affidavit back and forth across my grave.
No ordinary morning the morning

this morning; the morning the morning
was was wet and stunk of trodden flowers.
White screens overtowered our gabled house

this morning to contain the vacant hours
our remnant selves remained remaining in.
Of all mornings this morning stands

alone on its platform, hands on its head.
Undead, undead, undead.

Migration | NICOLE JIA MOORE

mum explains that when a human touches a baby bird its mother rejects it; i confess,
i walk my smell of tiger balm back to the tree anyway, chopstick in my hair too;
i think of bhanu kapil, who writes: it's exhausting to be a guest in somebody else's house
forever; my mum is a lady of science, so i use her mouth: the universe being infinite
there are many chances for our successes; she asks me to stay, then, and it's possible
we make the kitchen smell like nations while birds outside hit us with dreams;
there's many ways it could go;
mum asks me to stay, then, and we cry, and avoid the kitchen to sit with the birds; or else i
stay, and no one cries and i tell her about being labelled a stranger;
i stay, and don't even speak; just toss a coin and watch it spin up into the sky;
after dinner, mum walks me to the spot where gold dips back to us;
it's possible her watch is gold, or else
a trick of light; these days I bathe in milk;
in the shadows my skin is copper;
my mother is speaking
but her words are distant as birdsong; my father calls her
the *most exotic bird*
he ever held; how I wear his easy tongue and new name,
and kiss my mother, as any daughter does;

natural history poem | JONATHAN DUNK

tanned oxford dodo head Copenhagen 1847 moby dick's jawbone
vertical where for millions of years it had no predators ursus
arctos Belgium coalmine please don't touch the fucking bear
digging through bone suddenly rummaging in atavism for an
autochthonous reason not to find the t-rex underwhelming with
its stupid anæmic wings and grotesquely unnecessary
longvanished brickpit large & flightless like anyone else with
bidigital flightless sauric feet and a lot of unfathomably pointless
numbers homily erect flint ax and silicified conifer trunk necessity
somehow simultaneously blind and cruel and supposed I guess to
grope for some common amalgamate substrate linking the
megaloceros giganteus or some other Pleistocene fetish to the
meal deal from £3.99 open 7 00 to 20 00 and sightseeing and
what do these pious shortswearing pseudofucks think they
commune with writing their stupid fucking birdpoems but the
heaped abyssal history of the language we built we are to
slaughter raphus cucullatus and these other poor fucks and string
them here as icons of our conquest and the refined chandeliers of
genetic regret they think it pays for so they can come and write
and speak to our slaughter and think it has anything in common
though now perhaps it will in this last and the our of our death in
the coming not of spirit or capital but death as history's only
subject and what do they think they'll find
when they find it here

Notes on the After | DEREK CHAN
After Ada Limón

Not how it all wintered into scraps of half-inked

pear blossoms, nor how the pondwater never thawed

in time for the lotuses to proclaim their succulence

to the desperate Spring, it was the inscrutable loss of how

anything could begin afterwards which bowed me.

The clouds kept saying, *there will come a day*

when all of this blueness will be worth it.

The months when I couldn't tell if what hurt

was some unbreakable obsidian barb, or the hurt

of a growing, living thing. And it seemed almost pitiful,

how the frost clasped so closely to the birches;

sleeves of snow stitching the vastest grief

-coat ever conceived, entire fields suffocated

in a plead to be held. Only to be met by the soft

shock of winter unhinged at the speed it arrived, the music of held

breath returning from the scentless aftermath, wet hearts awakening

behind Spanish mosses, entire sunlit temples

of snail-shells unclouded along the highways.

How it was never about survival, but becoming

the patient rot beneath it all. Like the first of the fuchsias

now unfurling their infant flames on this patched,

uncertain earth; all of it rising for what we can't name.

On Not Cutting Through | BARRY HILL

Crossing the river Bug
I lay flat out on the barge
lowered the boom-mic down
to the forceful river
and had my ears rinsed in amber.

Such a wonder it was then.
All that I heard was so venerably ancient
I might have been re-born
into a peace that could heal the sodden fields
with their untold dead

Now it's happening again.
And I want to go back there once more.
Crazy, I know. What good could I do?
God does not help, no Buddhas help.
I have been telling my Zen friends as much.

Hang onto Lao Tzu, one says.
Start at chapter 29, and so on:
all that wisdom trying to govern
the world without force because force cannot win
when the world is a spiritual thing.

A musical thing? I almost said.
Oh, listen to the whistle in the missiles
their songs cannot be forced either.
Such a living and dying thing the world is.
Death flies all around us, over us, down on us.

Buddhistic drone that I am
I have landed in Kiev, I fly over rubble
frozen bodies in basements
and the ruins of the monument to Babi Yar.
I do a mindfulness walk along the avenue

made empty for the Russian tanks.
Gone, gone beyond, I chant, as they rumble in.
They won't shoot me, I play around
with inter-being itself, having called out
'This way to the gas, ladies and gentleman'.

Yes, I have no peace of mind
since my last visit to Poland.
What use my spirit in Ukraine?
Will I go to Odessa and see the opera house
for one last time? Their jewel facing a black sea.

But listen, have you heard about the cats?
At twilight they creep out of the rubble
for all the world like spiritual things.
They are taken in by brave men
with weapons on their shoulders.

The cats, as if they are kittens
curl up in the pockets of the heavy jackets.
Wild starving cats are tamed by the warmth.
They also sleep behind the knees of soldiers.
The soldiers sleep with vengeance in their hearts.

Lately, some have been found
shot by the side of the road, their hands tied.
What else do I know?
Many corpses are the off-spring
of the Cossacks who shot the geese, the Reds, the Jews…

And so on. As I write
The Russians seem to be retreating
having won the wrong way, as Lao Tzu said.
I cite Lao-Tzu for all the Straw Dogs he is worth.
What is anything worth? I ask a teacher.

He's still a young man, with a young family.
Life, he says, the emptiness teachings are to do with LIFE.
He knows I am nearly past it. In Kiev, I see him take up
arms to kill the troops who storm his basement!
No more Zazen!

Who am I to argue? The truth is neither
here nor there, it is nowhere clearly to be found
at least from here. Weapons are not auspicious tools
says Lao Tzu, some things are simply bad
So the man in my mind follows

all the railway lines of Ukraine. Again
he has passed Babi Yar, and, as a romantic gesture
in which he has no faith, he tries to imagine
a Diamond Sutra cutting through
to the opera house in his heart.

optimal | ALISON WHITTAKER

I pop a network of veins on my calf from
heaving my lardy murru up
a six to ten treadmill incline

I am advised to do this for
maybe an hour and eat
eighteen hundred calories (max) a day

I am minimising my health risks
as an Aboriginal woman

as an Aboriginal woman
from a long line of big yinarr
who must have died out of nowhere

excruciatingly and humiliatingly and
early and in public like I am now
for seven hours a week.

who must have died out of nowhere
and not because of a colony but
because they ate and drank and lived
sub-optimally as colonial subjects.

so I'm optimising.

---

on the treadmill   I find it hard to breathe,
or talk, so
sorry this po
em is so stilted   or

my legs tremble pursuing the gap

all I can think ab	out,		
aside from my p	endin g morta		lity,
(and ho w it's my	fault)		

is even more immi   nently shitting myse   lf,

    i eventually do in the gym bathroom
    i took a half bottle of
    Coloxyl 120. it looks like tar

I puke often, unrelated to the treadmill.

I go to see a dietician. I tell her about the vomiting
when I submit a diet plan. she says 'bulimics
usually know a bit more about nutrition.'

she points with a pen to my food diary 'see, rice crackers.'
I was disappointed because I ate them in the spirit
of optimisation. flavourless, portion-controlled.
a row is a hundred calories (max). she suggests keto.

on the way home I go by Sumo Salad. *ha.* a
woman takes my picture with her elbows
on a food court table and her shutter sound on.

I don't acknowledge it.
fatties aren't meant to show that we know.
or that we know that they know that we know.

whatever, I do all that *knowing, also keto, also speed*
until my liver pops out in weird x-ray
spots and all the weight I lost a *third of me* turns me

yellow so they pull out my gallbladder.
it was, the surgeon says, 'hmm, very bad'
and I'm high clot risk because of my fucked up calf veins

and also my teeth rot from their edges
from vomiting. I am given instructions to not
eat fats or too many carbs. on the way

home I go by the upper-gastro specialist
who took out my gall bladder, his office is
next to a sign about gastric sleeve weight loss
surgery. anyway, I'm crying out the front and another
fat girl takes my photo as the bus rolls by.

does she know *she's fat* and I know that
she knows *I'm fat* and that we know?
do I know if she knows that we're fat together? no.

I am reading some inquest findings.
in them I see many fat blak people pinned down
by scores of cops, people like me, who just
somehow spontaneously die of heart
failure because, randomly and out of
nowhere, their own big torsos were
'obscuring their airways' when they were
pressed flat into the ground
by a colony
for optimal control.

when I am arrested, they
take me to a pub bathroom
and make me piss with the door open.

I looked down at my foul and heaving belly,
which in its comorbid and racial risky mass is
covering my cunt and my dignity, and I think
a quiet and optimal 'thank you.'

Orphic Elegy V* | LUKE FISCHER

No-one expected
you would rise again
nor how or where
if it came to pass.
In abyssal night
you were woken by a cry,
a cry resounding
through underworld caverns.
It wasn't the cry of Eurydice
as viper fangs punctured her calf,
nor the cry of Pythagoras
condemned to Limbo for eternity,
nor the anguish of an infant
trapped in darkness. Not
of any human voice, the cry
of an animal, the last of its kind,
shook you with a cymbal's clamour
from the chasms of sleep, shattered
your core into a million shards
like sunlight on the coruscating sea.

The dying roar
of the last monk seal
crescendoed as it crossed
into the realm of shades. More
than an individual's despair, this cry
attested the death of a species, the end
of possibility of incarnation. As into a whirlpool,
into a black hole, the seal was retracted
into its idea, became a cousin
of the unicorn, a dream that would never again
wake in a supple body. And beyond the fate

of the Caribbean seal, it contained—in gong-like reverberations—
thousands upon thousands of tones and overtones,
each with its own coloured timbre.
With your ear attuned to the subtlest vibration
you divined spectres of vanished animals: a howling
Honshu wolf, a black-striped thylacine, a white-speckled river dolphin,
a hook-billed dodo, ridged lyre-horns of a Pyrenean ibex,
an ochre-breasted passenger pigeon, a pointy-nosed
pig-footed bandicoot, the long face and rack of a Caucasian elk,
a great auk standing upright on a stone, ink-marked wings
of a Madeiran butterfly matching a daisy,
black and white tattoos of a Caspian tiger
slinking between trunks of a phantom forest …
And the cry ever expanded
as Orpheus listened—wholly exposed—
to the cacophony of pain, irreparable loss.

Meanwhile a tree arose on your left side—
arose from the underworld's sterile, grey soil—
and branched into a lyre with tightly-strung tendrils.
As you plucked them, they sent forth sounds
clearer than the pure-tongued syllables of rocky springs
and modulated the chaos: the metallic clash and thunderous
echoes subdued into tones of flute and violin,
adjusted to the lyre's tonic, arranged themselves
into patterns, bright chords, constellations,
remembered rhythms of breath, pulse and walk,
gestation and flight. And as planets weave
colours through the circle of animals,
join them in a mobile text, you wove
a dream in song: *Gathered together*
in the kingdom of the dead, we sing in service

to the source of life. Once my voice paved a path—
each word a stepping-stone—downwards from the world
and across the river of forgetting, but now with all of you
who cannot return to the sun's abode or gather
under a canopy's dome, my voice seeks a path to the ears
of the living, to touch their hearts as once it found entrance
to the cold heart of Hades. We sing with the hope that humans
may hear, may find in the roar of the dying seal, the fire
of this song, the fire of determination to end the devastation,
a future harmony of all elements and beings,
the double choir of the living and the dead, remembering each other
in antiphon from both sides of the river.

* This poem is the final part of a poetic sequence addressed to Orpheus, which travels from antiquity to the present.

Penstock Lagoon | SARAH DAY

Central Highlands, Tasmania, January 2022

We wake by still water
to what sounds like a large pearl dropped from a great height,
it breaks the surface tension with a resonant nasal tock
more than a splash.

This lake is nine hundred and sixty-three metres
above sea level. It is a metre deep.
Up here, in the tent at night, by an effort of will,
the world's troubles shrink from the mind's large screen
to something smaller that glows dimly in the dark as I sleep:
for the moment it features a satellite image of Russian troops
gathering on the border of Ukraine.

Snow seems to settle more heavily where the razed Yelnya forest
has made way for lines of trucks, artillery, tanks.
The impression from space is monochrome.

At dawn the rising sun sets the tent's orange interior ablaze.

Black swans are waking in the distance with dented bugle calls.
Still, from time to time, the pearl falls and tocks
and still the small screen flickers at the back of the mind:
young men, boys, in great-coats, cold-faced to the camera
in freezing trenches.

I remind myself that this is not 1914.
I think of the rubble of Homs,
and wonder at the satisfaction victory brings.

It is not a falling pearl but a musk duck.
No-one but us—least of all the morning—
is startled by the oddity:
the black galleon of its profile,
the huge lobe beneath its bill,
the pure, surreal music of its one brief note, falling,
the spirals of waterdrops from wingbeats.

Nearly two and a half thousand years ago
Thucydides wrote: *It is a common mistake
in going to war to begin at the wrong end,
to act first and wait for disaster to discuss the matter.*

Despite the vagaries of good and evil
the imagination insists on connections.
With the Ukrainian soldiers, for example,
the Russian soldiers, the Ukrainian people.

Mirror-like, on its ancient glacial plateau,
the lake is non-partisan in its view of civilisations.

Mayflies are hatching on its surface for their single day of life.

peptalk | JOANNE BURNS

peptalks two bob a penny let
the tictac do the math but nothing
prepared your palate for that mega
jab the extracted teeth now sleeping
like tiny dogheads in a cellophane pack
like [or unlike] the exhumed richard the
third in a british carpark a tongue curls back
a cautious caterpillar disoriented in a mouth's
intimate history as the bloodgates refuse to
close & not much clear memory to probe –
un-like a virgin abscessed
tooth extraction on the cusp
of a teenage confirmation at sin
city's sombre cathedral where you
swore to the cardinal not to let
alcohol pass your lips for at least
eight years a swig of aged renée
royal brandy resting on the carpet
beneath a book on oulipo might
do the trick right now does this taste
like a poem ~

Photograph: Sunday with Joy, carrying Sweeney at Heide
| EMILIE COLLYER

His echo is in the garden
baby shape immortalised

a fat bundle hip-nestled
side of Joy's face is Sun lit

there are issues with wombs
how to carry a child

within and without
(so many ways mothers fail)

                                  some mammalian
                                  species practice cooperative

                                  breeding: meerkats
                                  Ethiopian wolves, primates, humans.

Joy births Sweeney
hands care to Sunday

who can't have children
dotes on a doll called Gethsemane

immortalised by Joy
in gouache and ink on paper

                                  some animals
                                  abandon offspring

                                  pandas often birth
                                  twins but only have enough

                                  milk for one
                                  snakes lay eggs and glide away.

Efforts made by aching skin
to hold what can be held

it stretches
sometimes ruptures

                his echo in the garden
                the small hut

                his barrelling life—ended short
                speculations as to what

                was damaged in him
                (within and without)

                                gardens—even beautiful ones—
                                can be sites of betrayal

things fall through that
can't always be retrieved.

Pikes Peak | SARAH HOLLAND-BATT

Hiking near the timberline at twelve thousand feet
my father mistakes an almost silent stroke for vertigo—
immobilisation that arrives like a tsunami,
the body withdrawing to its furthest reaches,
brain stem stoppered for a paralysing second.
He sits winded in a rubble of rose granite
staring at the infinite regression of quaking aspen,
valley after valley to the horizon,
stunned by his own elevation. Then fear,
comprehension: he has lost the language
for water, aspirin. An icy breeze shearing
off snow, heads of spruce and bristlecone
stretching all the way down to the switchback
roads where motorcycles lean in terminal arcs.
At this height everything grows deformed
by wind and cold—flag trees with a single comb
of greenery down a leeward side,
krummholz pines twisted into pretzel bends,
scratchings of alpine parsley, dwarf clover.
Who knows exactly when it started or was over—
a lightning storm in the skull, its barometer
registering no drop in pressure—then whole zones
denuded like the palms after Castle Bravo—
detonation raising storeys of ocean to the sky.
I gave myself a fright, he says, and shakes his head—
a bull shifting a cloud of horseflies.
Around my father tundra grass is blowing
grain by stunted grain. This is the vista
about which Katharine Lee Bates wrote *America
the Beautiful*—only line of which I ever remember

is *O beautiful for pilgrim feet,* which to me
means precisely zero. But if I strain I can still see him
sitting dumbfounded in that field of feldspar,
his beautiful pilgrim feet laced into white Reeboks and gym socks
as a sunburst ripples through his brain.
My father is calm as a monk whose long meditation
produces imperceptible shifts
in his physiognomy, and I understand
he went up the mountain for the same reason
everyone goes up mountains.
He went up the mountain to change.

Poem for my Ancestors | EILEEN CHONG

Write for your people, they tell me.

My people of the river delta.
My people of the crossed seas.

Northern people who became
Southern people—*no people*

*

My people who lost their language.
My people carved out new worlds.

Grandfathers of grandfathers:
illegible words in a ledger.

The order of misspelled names
written wrong on all the forms.

I call these names in the night.
My people, I cry. *My people—*

There is no answer.
They are long cold in the earth.

They are far beyond any communion.

*

There was no funeral like my grandmother's.
Nothing went up in smoke except for her body.

No blankets embroidered with Chinese
characters hung up like before. Even

the crematorium had a facelift—the soft
glow of lamps, the inside cavernous with pews.

At the front, no cross or altar: just space, and the furnace.

*

A family on a boat. Ashes in a bright
red bundle. Prayers, a Buddhist monk,

his rung bell. The hour her ashes were released
into the sea, we were in the ocean, the water

sucking at our feet. We looked across to the horizon.
All bodies of water are connected, I lied. *She is with us now.*

Her hand cold in mine as she cried for her mother.

*

A magpie one day; a currawong the next.
Cockatoos screamed and wheeled away.

Which bird was her spirit made manifest?
No song I heard turned into dream.

The cuckoo in the red clock nodded to the hours.

*

We arrived in the rain, and drove for miles
away from the city. Outside the cemetery gates,

we gathered handfuls of wild daisies. The sun
burned in the thin sky. Headstones like giant

crusted fingertips thrust from beneath the earth.
He stopped: *my grandparents*—I bent to place

the flowers at their graves, and pulled at the weeds.
Nettles stung my hands, and I cried out in pain.

He nodded. *It's Tommy and Senga, saying they see you.*

*

A single mahjong tile: mouth shot through
with a spear; a globe spinning on its axis.

Her kitchen in my kitchen; her hands ghostly
on mine. We feed the ones we love. We scrape

our bowls clean. We scrub them white as bone.

*

What does it mean for a life
when you know you will be no one's ancestor?

Hungry every waking minute. We count
the ribs of prisoners-of-war. Bloodlines

blurred like ink on crumpled, clutched tickets.

*

Someday a girl will read this and think
of survival. Another girl once climbed

a mud wall and escaped into the night,
carrying only two pilfered buns

and a fragment of jade from her mother.
She did not know where she would end up.

She began in darkness so I might become light.

poem for protection | ELLEN VAN NEERVEN

what comes first the poem or the poet
which remains longer on Country

poem, please protect me from greed
danger occurs when I crave the singular

hiding in the crackle of the present
crave, the sandalwood behind the neck

in the quiet corners of the room
behind the ears of hugs

quiet, the earth moves so greatly
when I want to run

remain originated by soul
move, scoot, nothing

while we still have hours
souls, to the big block of wind

I am a living line   I am a living line
I stay in the light in the light I stay in the light in the light

The Portable Home | SABA VASEFI

Once, I went with the wolf to the desert
to take back honey from the bear
but in town my two eyes counted
only for one. At school
the only colours allowed
were black, brown, navy or grey.
To make a Muslim of me,
they hid me in a chador.
No matter how many holy verses
they made my mouth express,
no prayers found their God.
I did not capitulate;
with the heat of my eyes
I incinerated the gates
of hell!

When I was seven, to console my
tears for the many forbidden colours,
my grandmother told me under a fig tree,
the sky is the same colour
wherever you are.
When I was twenty-eight,
I auctioned my kitchen garden
to fly to a forest,
yearning to burn
under an azure sky.

I find solace
now, though I stand naked,
stripped of the dour colours
when the Persian sky
did not know my name—
Though this raucous sky
is not kind to me,
not savvy to my skin.
Tehran was a hoarfrost
on my lips; Sydney
is a cockatoo scream in
my stateless mouth

and the world a
Tower of Babel.

I have tried insanity,
I have taken every pill,
even the moon, I swallowed!
The ocean I swim is blue,
but not the blue
of the Caspian Sea.
I am the blue desert,
a pomegranate in bloom.
The broken seeds are
fragments in my mouth.
I am a memoir in blood.
The ink of all existence
is the colour of the sky
and exile is a horizon[1] without end.
Salvation beckons
like a lunar eclipse.
I have travelled the clouds
to change the sky's mood,
but it stays unmoved—
I want to bring the moon to the ground.

Within me
I would fashion a portable home;
wherever I go
I live nowhere.
Between the inhale and
exhale of my expatriate breath,
I ask God to lift his feet
so I can mop under my desk.
He was my prison,
but I'm always a woman
with a body in the wilderness;
not a prisoner in a tent.

---

[1] 'Horizon of Exile' is an installation by Isabel Rocamora.

prayer for the parents of every addict | SCOTT-PATRICK MITCHELL

ahem

meat emanate
that heat
him, imp
aim pin
inmate, hit it
animate anthem
pant aphanite
eat ten het men
attain mania
methane mane
heap teeth
ante mint
theme thin
team tinea tin
name paean   paint Pan
patient
patinae, pain, maim

methamphetamine, emit hate
meme at heathen me
i   am   them:
mime; manatee; mine; meanie;
a meth matinee;
the pi hi eaten meatpie;
pieman; hitmen; apeman; titmen;
an amme heap, anti-neat;
inept nap;
hath tine tip.

pa
ma
mama
tempt teatime
nip amphetamine neap
tame pent pen
tie thine time titan
then theta tap

ai

amen

Pumping Station | ISI UNIKOWSKI

Bowler-hatted, unsmiling, moustachioed,
a group of men stands beside their machines;
apprentices crouch at their feet, caps awry as their grins.
The manager's wife flaunts the region's first car.
In these huge posters by the ticket office,
it's easy to mistake the time the shutter took to descend
for gravitas, as if watching us.

Once inside, the polished, gleaming semi-darkness makes
the glare barricaded at the entrance look cheap and flat.
Huge pistons are poised, about to resume
their genuflections, giant flywheels stationary beside them
as though the parts of some celestial clockwork
had been dismantled and lined up.

The guide balances a coin on the casing
to show how smoothly the piston rods perform,
without the least vibration, in greased silence.
Our kids, from a world of few moving parts,
where whatever machinery is left
is so well-hidden it might as well be magic,
go back outside for better reception, unimpressed,

but we linger out of curiosity:
for all the size of these components,
there was an amenable logic
and purpose to the way rocking beams, cranks, rods
moved and pulled and pushed, visibly connecting
to the task or purpose
of lifting and conveying the most basic elements of a city
from one place to a much better place

and nostalgia too, for the reticent confidence
in machinery tooled with such precision,
yet still decorated, made beautiful in filigree and ornament
as though sludge had its sacral moments too
for all the boilers' black, bulky
indestructibility; to make a machine
that could operate with such grace,
as if all that was needed to keep the world in motion
was someone in overalls proudly standing by
with a little can of oil.

Purgatory | JUDITH CRISPIN

I can't sleep here,
in this curve of the East Baines River—
too much blood on the ground,
and my campfire throws a mottled light
over mulga, burnishing insects,
and filling this changeling night with forms.

When it's humid like this,
sound travels.

Crocodiles barking
in the creek behind the van park, somewhere
a car radio plays Bowie:
     for we're like creatures of the wind,
        and wild,
           wild is the wind.

On these banks, boabs
hold stars between their fingers
like splintered bone—
their torsos are globes, carved
with images of snakes and the names
of those shot while dancing ceremony,
on a night just like this, a night split
by rifles—the first crack
erupts the egrets
from the river's
 still surface.

A century is nothing for boabs.

These roots remember
the warm weight
of babies, pushed by their mothers
into blackness and the living smell of mud—
how they slipped
through water's dark like creatures
of wind and wild is
my breath

becomes the sound of water hissing
through roots, snakes carved
in a boab's skin,
like the snake that comes to me in dreams
speaking her language of coagulants,
blood venom, neurotoxins.

Lightning eddies through the interior of clouds—
a dangerous lightning,
opening like wings
or branching nerves—and in its light,
all those drowned babies are gliding
above the river,
their slow heads turning
to hold me, in their savage windburned gaze.

Time to go.

I wake the dog, upend a billycan on the fire.
A few minutes to pack the ute, and we drive east
into landscape cloaked in Witchetty—
and the boabs follow,
burning their way out of form.
I carry them as sparks in my iris,
in the familiar sea-green lights of the dash,
as min-min racing beside the road.

One eye on the rear-view mirror,
East Baines River vanishes
into the reach of mountains.
The last boab
is a great, dark octopus
silhouetted against stars.
A bellbird drops from its branches as we pass,
arcing noiselessly into headlights,
its western wing,
its wild and shining eye.

quandongs | MAYA HODGE

I peel and peel quandongs in my mothers garden.
    The ice in my water melts slowly onto the hot surface of our scuffed wooden table. I watch as the light gently slides across the shed wall telling me the time is slowly moving on by.
As I peel the quandongs black gunk sticks to my fingernails and scatters across my lap.
    I want to dry my quandongs in the sizzling Mildura afternoon heat
    To let the skin glisten like blood-red tree sap.
        I want the fruit to curl in the exquisite sun
        I want the skins to cook so I can breathe it deep into my lungs.
        We reach up high to pick and pick the quandongs.
        I remember when I was a little girl hiding amongst the saltbush watching my mother and aunties pick and pick quandongs.
        In the sweltering sun they gathered the fruit in time with the honeyeaters song.
I sit and softly wash the fruit. Trying to get the infestation out.
Trying to stop the invasion of bugs that chew and chew until the fruit is rotten to the core.

My bare back hot from the stern eye of
the sun and my tired feet flat against the
concrete floor.

Peeling back time as I sit with my
mother.

Picking and picking quandongs along the long
winding river of this Country's spine.

Keeping a loving eye on the seasons and the scar tree filled
with native bees.

We walk mother and daughter along the banks of the river and the dense
curtain of river-reeds.

I pull the seeds from the quandongs and pile them in bowls on our kitchen table.
Sometimes I still find them hidden in the shadows of my pockets.

They overflow in our home and rest in the coolomon sitting beneath our living
room mantel.

I want to boil the fruit in brown sugar and let it slowly turn into soft sunset
silken syrup.

The colour of the rolling sand dunes
and the Country that nourished me.

As I sit and peel and peel
quandongs.

In my mothers garden.

Rain | GLENN MCPHERSON

1.
If there is capacity for illusion, rain like this, at spring's end,
Bringing down a chill from the mountains out of season

Is beautiful in the jacaranda flowers,
Like a colony of seals over the footpath on a singular

Gulag of hope. A chill appropriated,
Like beauty, is an act of benevolence,

To walk in this is to bow one's head.

2.
After making love there are times that ice sets
In. When it sets out a time, unacclimatised to flame,

We are closer then, to the wonder of death.
Something halts, a shadow, a cultivation yielding

Once again to the blackbird,
Some spirit by spring waters between us.

3.
Indiscriminate aggregation born on the hips
Of grave stones, and sidewalks unnamed,

From relentless rain, carry no protest over the suburbs,
Over the vast grey sea threshing;

The blind scurry of all those who hold earth;
Over wrested light thrown up

By car after car after car…

4.

At what point confession becomes destructive
Shall be left aside, obliged in an instant
With the duty of creation. The vapour
That brought the consecration of shrouds
Is smelled upon arrival. Black leaves, stem,
White petals collected of their immense
Ghosts speak through the strip of old carpet
Lifted from an overgrown lot
Holding fast for the god's
Use again, but for now, by an old drum,
Under the silver rags of a birch grove,
A foot or more of coal and dark smoke
Stiffen it for sleep, on the shoulders of a peasant.
Her face numinous in the spleen coloured eve.

5.

Words tumble on and on in all
Pentecostal tongues
Out of storm drains crudely stuffed
With the syntax of leaves, while ravens
Descend and ascend with Bach on their wings
In one long, continuous mass.

6.

If it were to end here the ground would soon dry,
Leaving echoes of water as ellipses

For an alchemist or astrologist to refine. They would see
The disappearance of winter, feel

The burden of perfection interfered with and
Know how to equate.

There is a low moon the colour of rusted iron
Breaking, at intervals, through waxen clouds:

And it's not the end, though some fissure drags
Like iron filings, great streaks of bats.

Tonight I will lose a daughter in my sleep
And drink the lake dry to find her.

She will have caught the golden fish,
Her face petrified in chastity, and will weep for what is in me.

recline | DAVID STAVANGER

openings can be challenging
where to sit everyone who has a chair named after them

opera chair from investment banking requires ergonomics
being chair of an arts org is both pleasure and responsibility

[chair now an object, now belonging to or associated with person]
not everyone can be given the name of a monarch

      I enter my name into a chair name generator
      it asks me what I currently do in life
      (I work in an office/I do not work in an office)
      how often I work out will assist in calculating a title
      whether I see infrastructure as big or small

there is an art to naming furniture, there is more at stake
than any new born child due to levels of production

seeking visceral connection with consumers
everybody wants a throne, nobody dignifies a toilet

IKEA has the process down to a science
all have Scandinavian origins

      beds have Norwegian place names; seating have Swedish ones
      in my next life I will return as a Stavanger queen ensemble
      I will be a port to strangers' dreams
      a berth for bodies, ferrying the traffic of pleasure boats
      paying tribute to cruise administration

no mentions of chairs were made in the bible
(the more you rely on a backrest, the more you tend to slump)

companies fund chairs as part of good corporate citizenship
(Jesus was not a good corporate citizen, he liked to stand up)

billionaire is padded soft beige eco-leather with vintage walnut structure
(just one in 10 ASX 200 chairmen is a woman)

      I sit in this lounge chair and watch the first season of shows
      I sit on this swivel chair and preside over search engines
      (look up things with a back and four legs that can't walk)
      dream of a chair to carry the day weight of dreaming
      I up look up dream chair online and become two inches of foam

a well-endowed chair requires chutzpah
catbird seat is the best place to chew the ear off a president

as Ellen DeGeneres says *Leaning forward in your chair*
when someone is trying to squeeze behind you isn't enough

we will break down before the office chair, these bare ends
not built to comprehend how many of us there really are

      microplastics have been found lodged deep
      in the tissue of living people for the first time.
      there is increasing concern about hazards within us.
      we have each swallowed the equivalent of one hundred stackable chairs,
      our lungs are an auditorium of unsustainable applause.

Rendezvous | BROOK EMERY

Even standing still it's flickering this way and that,
the mind, that dematerialised, invisible thing,
swaying like a ship's light in a storm,
picking out memories, slights, landmarks
which may not exist at all, plotting a future
which may never come. I hear it talking secretively,

flipping from labyrinth to waterfall to field of wheat,
from scorpion to red-bellied black to tangled thicket
and fast flowing stream already threatening
to break its banks: feather, wing, teetering branch,
a cavity beneath a hollow log, teeming insect life.
The mind, that uncertain interlinear thing

weaving between and through the clouds,
rumbling thunder, sheet lightning, and the after-image
which effloresces behind closed lids:
sun shower, followed by deluge, drizzle,
footprints in wet grass, the dissolving life of mud,
the tramp who leaves never/always to return.

The mind, that imagined, un-located thing,
ringing on and off like an unanswered phone—
please leave a message—the unconnected
farrago of clicks and tones, the breathy pause,
exhalations and exasperations, a night sky
constellation of comets and dying stars.

The mind, a late night stop on a country road,
the dashboard lights turned low, the radio
a fuzz of static, the engine idling and revving
spasmodically; on the passenger seat an empty wallet,
an envelope, a child's drawing of a gun; the misted windows
framing a time and place for the rendezvous.

Requiem (fire) | DAVID BROOKS

On the 26th of October last year, five a.m.,
I heard, for half an hour, an unfamiliar bird-call
and tried to record the shape of it
in my notebook in the bedroom dark.
At 10.55 that morning, meteorologists now say,
a bolt of lightning from a dying storm
struck a bone-dry stringy bark
deep in that part of the national park
they call the Devil's Wilderness,
igniting a fire that burned unreachable through the day.
At 7.10 our beloved dog Charlie, riddled with cancer, struggled
to his feet beside our outdoor table
and tried to get inside. We picked him up
and took him to his place beside the bed.
Five minutes later, as if some large invisible creature
had placed their knee in the middle of his spine
and, hand beneath his jaw, pulled him
backwards like a longbow, he reared
then bent slowly forward
and took no further breath. By the middle
of that night the fire
had burned five hundred hectares. Un-
stoppable through November, December, January, it became
the largest bushfire Australia's ever seen. No
human died but no-one knows
how many animals it killed; day after day whole
flocks of birds incinerated in mid-flight; day after day
whole families of wallabies, wombats, possums
outrun by flame. Burnt leaves and embers
fell from the air. There were fires across town, fires
on our own road. Our bags were packed. We lived
in constant readiness, but what is that? I said
goodbye to books, to photographs, to papers, gave
in my mind
so much of my life away
it seemed I'd found a new lightness
like a second, fire-hardened skin, astonished yet again

at how little our vast lives boil down to; each of us
confronting our essential isolation, walking through.

When at last it came, the heavy rain
that extinguished the exhausted blaze
almost on our doorstep turned our lower acre
into an image of the Zambezi River. That
was early February; four weeks later
the virus had come; my being
one of those at risk, we spent the next
eight months completely shut away. I've not
gone to the fire ground
but—gang gangs, whistlers—watched refugees come.

It's
spring now, fire
season again. Last week
my young granddaughter, wearing
a red fire-jacket and hard plastic hat,
led me out to the garden to see
the blaze on the bottlebrush, the purple
torches of lavender, the deep crimson blooms
of the camellia, knocked to the ground by the wattlebirds
and smouldering in the thick new grass,
saying *shshsh, shshsh* as she pulled the trigger
of her magic extinguisher, putting out each flame.

It's
Spring, October, cicadas
are tunnelling up from the roots of the cherry tree, ducklings
fossick in the vegetable beds, the sheep
need shearing, the lemons
are bright over Charlie's grave.
This morning
I heard that bird again.
I still don't know its name.

Rezoning | JOHN KINSELLA

'Bergère ô tour Eiffel le troupeau des ponts bêle ce matin'
—Apollinaire

False praise lights up the launch site, O delivery vehicle.

The delivery zone is empty but investors have no crisis of relevance
and couldn't care less—deliveries are taking place
elsewhere and will continue until the cows come home—

there's metal-dust on the water vats, the hand-sanitiser dispenser
is exhausted or ignored. Rezoning the bushland for places of worship
where bushland is a place of worship is a key to whose paradox?
You don't need the dark web to purchase a skeleton key as they're
available via adverts beneath online television guides: in plain sight.

The phone tower has blended with *landscape*—tallest tree on top
of the hill admired or ignored by those travelling in hertz rental waves.
Satellites are the Roc image of cascading truths, but where is the passion
of a God's eye view, the shepherds mulesing the sheep—traumatised
bleats and a virtual life, well, elsewhere. Remember, those anti-pastorals
published in Cuba brought on a conversation of tangents.

Working the genealogy into a frenzy, feeling the sun probe
the factor seventy, repairing fences to work as two-way mirrors,
locating the cloud within the cloud to counteract the forecast—
psalms of endgame splashed about as memory.

Or turning away from visible streets, you might think to find solace
in a box of discarded records only to find they are littered with discs
from skinhead neo-Nazis bands, causing a rupture in the lucky dip
of materialism, the aesthetics of fatalism. And so, the geranium
flowering affects people passing in so many different ways,
their political affiliations and anxieties finding less correlation
in facial expressions, the touchscreen correspondences.

Each eulogy of mass-communication lauds its own modes of travelling.
Easily said by someone so glib, you might say? The red flowering gum
is over the line, the other side, and yet we see and smell its influence—
I travel nowhere now after travelling as if it were a right,
which is not the same. A fantail flew in front of the car
and I braked suddenly, in time, a wagtail did the same
a few kilometres later and I missed that as well.

Such is the irony of travel and heavy industry, but that was locally,
which we might say is not the same. How many points on the globe
accrued in moment and result? I am just saying. Or you are just asking.
What is the point of coming inside if you don't salute the pollen,
the loose leaves, swirling of sand, the carapace of a dead beetle curling.

Testing of sewerage shows up fragments of virus. *Strong indicators.*
And wide-usage of methamphetamines. And so much *else*?
Rivals for dominance of space exploration occupy the same space
as rivals for dominance of space. Music selected for voyages.
They wish to refill the Hadron emptiness. Exhausted by a future,
they are rezoning the spiritual in more ways than one—plethoras.
Some have contracts to offer as proof. Others have tenders
to show they believe in absolute self-belief. The dying can't breathe.

        Who am I with my alternative up-bringing?
        Who am I with my murky personal history?
        Who am I to shade in the blanks in a colour-
        by-numbers that reveals a hawk that isn't
        a hawk?
                City streets traversed to know a city
        for all its change as we lapse, starving
        on replays. You could update via 'streetview',
        but phantom memories seem not to counter
        a short-circuit. Empirically smart buildings glint,
        gorging themselves into those Pyrrhic sunsets, wasted dawns.

The cutting of the sun's throat is a threat made by weapons-researchers
beyond closed doors of their 'personal lives'. As if secretive activities
can be separated from behaviour of, say, *in the home*. This is entangled
with patriotism, isn't it? Being so different from watching a sparrowhawk
to learn more about its ways of processing errors, taking a non-lethal
interest in its fluctuations. The movie star can join the party of double-
standards, and millions of sceptics and believers will watch collaterally.

I've heard peacocks calling to close out a day, perching high
in pepper trees, retracting their displays to fit—I never saw eyes
I saw punctuation marks. And as for the lyre-bird, it mimics
a different side of the continent and sounds off the spectrum
of colours here—warning and comfort, distraction and assurance.
A lyre and a bird are at risk from foxes at risk from shooters.

Ah, disbeliever saying prayers methodically.
Discount the biography, accolades, self-permissions,
promises of deliverance, a place in the aftermath.

The monastery fantasy of devotion is a safe house of isolation?
Casting stones at light-collecting surfaces, or comfortable
in the choices you are able to make?

Who will scribe the ruins of investment?
Who will mimeograph when spare parts fail?
Who will illustrate the cold(ness) clichés of space
making the keepers so hot under their collars?
Who will scry the contradictions for their own silences?
Who will sign the documents of renunciation?
Who will give up what they have extracted
no matter how much they damn that extraction?

Aren't these issues of writing? Of the shaping or malformation of script?
Aren't these turnings of notation? How to write 'without prejudice',
without weighting the tones? Atonal pitchforks descaling the walls
of centralised power. We hope to accumulate our loves and gather
love safely? Remember the unimpressive view on the busier
side of a hill, heading down to the stunning but oil-polluted bay.

Remember the chromatics of migrant birds affording your(self)
the luxury of seeing where they left and where they've arrived,
doing so much more work than you. Cells. How many can we lose
to the phrase? Rural land zoning as malleable as extraction—animal
husbandry, 'forestry' and 'natural resource management'. Notice the drills
reaching deep under the paddocks: zoning will cope with greenwash
that will gush out like power from lithium batteries.

We document from remnant vegetation: eye to the knothole,
galah watching on from the loveheart-shaped opening
to its annual nesting hollow, knowing 'temporary' is a mining company's
demi-secret password. Knowing 'diversity' is a definition of a workforce,
a demographical lexicon without breadth for exchange, for challenges
to its authority. Who is in this travelogue? What is noted in decorative
acts, the collecting and collating across hemispheres?

Farewells conditional on leisuretime. The culturally
unfamiliar adorning new pages of self-affirmation,

shared visionless, hackers with bells on

polarised, or senses

dulled.

Rivers | YEENA KIRKBRIGHT

Three rivers run
in my blood, where my mother takes
me home, where mud lives between toes, and rain
is a creature that transforms before my eyes, into river water
falling from rocks into my blood, stepping
carefully along Country, breaking
it gently as it does.

Here where I river-float
with my ancestor brother. I make ripples
he doesn't. We're laughing at Dad, tellin again
how *Billabong* comes from a Wiradjuri word. Old man crow
is eyein us from the banks. We know it's
Grandfather tellin us youngfullas
"Respect your Elders."

This River is old
like Earth's granite bones
endorheic and slowing, for marsh lovers
reed weavers, for migratory mob. This River flows
old magic backwards from sea, makes saltwater
spirits in freshwater
shallows.

This river
is swollen with matriarchy
she's boiling, flooded and cold
she jumps dams, eats earth with insatiable hunger, dumps fish
on front lawns, puts a couch in the tree
tells the kids "Get in
here NOW!"

This river
inhales and exhales
with the tides, she is connected to the rhythm
of all things, pulled and pushed by the gravity of dark matter
she flows where she wants, grows where she wants
and menstruates mud
along coastline.

River's name is
changed from *the place where*
Brolgas played to the name of a man who once
owned a company, a company that changes the shape
of the river, bares Country of bush
makes it barren
and used.

This English language
is full of polite words for things
that are violent. Ownership. Colonisation.
Non-consensual. Stolen. Dredging. Damming. Irrigation.
Mining. Aqueduct. Rape. River sleeps this year.
Sleeps deep. Where river?
Here river.

My river, my river
my river is a finger of universe
pointing, is spring-fed, is snowmelt
is rain-filled, is flesh warmed on bones, is Country
knowing, flowing, flooding, my river
my body, your river, our body
soon may be gone

Ruby* | DR CHELINAY GATES AKA MULARDY

I can see ya ... Looking at me.
I know your friends have gone
But still your heart is here.
Where them cherubs sang and shed a tear
For youse blackfellas staying here.

I can see ya ... It's okay my friend.
Although you didn't know me then.
I love You now
As if our love has always been.

I can see ya ... Ruby Nugweea
I'm going outside
Come, put your hand in mine.
I'll show ya where them fellas laid ya body
When ya died.

I can see ya Ruby ... ya smiles as broad as mine
Ya hand's so warm and kind.
And ya fingers are so long and fine.
So this is "it", dear Ruby?
This little cross, your shrine?

I can see ya ... it's okay to cry.
Let me pick them yellow flowers.
I'll add a Boab leaf or two
And tie it up with strands of my grey hair.
This bouquets just for you.

I can see ya ... your life's been real tough.
You arrived at just 11 and died at 37.
A leper most your life.
Were they kind to you out here?
Were your nights filled with fear?

I can see ya ... Ruby, ya know I have to go.
Them shadows are growing mighty long.
The sunsets too quickly here in Bungarun.
That white-fella won't stop beepin' his horn.
'Til I get get in that van ... then we'll be gone.

I can see ya ... through the whirling dust as he drives off.
Ya standing in the graveyard beside that little cross.
Howling at the top of your voice. "Come back! Come back!"
Them words break my heart in two.
There's too much time and space between me and you.

I can see ya ... Clutching them yellow flowers and boab leaf bouquet.
And that chunk of my heart that broke-off with grief that day.
In my dream I hear ya whisper, "one day I'll take you far away".
Those words I scrawled so long ago in that blood red dirt
Was my promise that I'd return for you ... my friend
Ruby ... The Lonely Ghost of Bungarun.

*Written at the abandoned Bungarun Leprosarium in Derby WA.

The Saltpan | YASMIN SMITH

I am grilling the gills of mackerel
where their bodies line up
like salt-dipped lungs.
I am licking salty plum fingers
under the mangrove roots
of shallow reef and mud.

When the coral cleanses itself
the colour of coconut flesh
covers the coastal strike from eye to eye,
and sulphurous feet
remap the home
of my grandmother's mother.

Winter has come as pink and cyan
sitting at borders with one another.
Yellow-crested
cockatoos peak
perched at the top of the pine,
spitting splinters of cone
on our skulls
and the tidal moon
stays cold, at midnight.

In the fire pit we cling
to cockleshells and hymns,
brew bitter tealeaf in liquorice coal.
The after-thought
of sweet potato skins
unfurling beneath our fingertips.

Inside the canopy
where my sister sleeps
under mosquito gauze,
I too, look for you,
where once
I found the pit of a peach
in the papasan
shaped like a wentletrap.

I return your body in August,
sweet melon, pale iris
tapioca, harpoon.
You sleep in
the vacant undertow
with scalloped eyes and catfish hues.

I split the skin underfoot
on shucks of oyster shell,
breathe in the rim of the saltpan,
and wash my feet
in early prayer.

Salt Water Kin | JILL JONES

As water turns & returns   it changes from
    ocean   ground   & sky   onto
these beachside rocks   as I taste salt water
    kin of saliva   (a memory of exploring rock pools)

I look into today's pools   they're swirled clear
    or gathered with irritant   like pearl

as surge catches in sandstone   sings hollows
    where submerged grasses weep
posidonia sinuosia   heterozostera tasmanica

*

What is a wave but a moment   & a continuum
    in wordless language   swell   pitch   break
shaping its cold sweat on our cars   our skin
    as the city rolls into the gulf   abandoned water bottle
in the tide's reach

*

Stray sky water falls on my cheek
    the truest fragment may be a rain drop
even if not transparent   it carries so much
maybe some days are grey for a reason

as this present fills up with pasts   sea past
    bird past   fish trails   rain history   in clouds
vapour   brine   erosions   cinders of trees & ice
    tasting bitter   like everything we've had to swallow

like crust   of the pink lake we once passed
    clapped out memory of a green shore   slurries &
shams hunched on cracked industrial edges

*

The sea has no nostalgia   its currents
    undo everything   strew & scrape   leavings
of the extinct   some things fresh

icecream wrapper   old bricks turned to pebbles
    new washed shells   plastic in forever colours
worn wood   cuttle bone

Today, seagulls steal garbage from our hands
we shout 'hey, here'   by the lagoon
    sandhills   the pier   as landscapes stretch
from us   watery   dry   across the world

Will the clear water return?

*

Until everything silts up   this is what we do
    cup water to our mouths   & spill it
    for ground   write in this salt   fresh   tongue
turn over its ancient syllables   without drowning

Scar Tissue | ES FOONG

You lead me through strange geographies.
You say, up here the tide
cannot drown our sandwiches.
You say, up here you can see
where salt scarred the land.
I tell you, my steps follow
your footfalls.
I don't say, I can only drink
where the rocks have cut my veins.
I don't say, here:
I am a snail without my shell.

You lead me to new territories.
You say, all our wandering lives
we have trained for thinner air.
You say, sun fire will not scar
the brave.
I tell you, my steps follow
your footfalls.
I don't say, I am invisible
without the waves to speak my shape
I don't say, ash has filled my mouth
and I cannot breathe.

Scarred Landscape | BRENDA SAUNDERS

The plane flies low over a curve of red ochre country. Landforms scatter. A waterhole stretches the horizon. Trees flash by in a line of grey. My window lifts to frame the sky, dips to saltpans turning blue after rain. The perspective tilts, pulls a mine into focus. Moving like ants, giant loaders dredge the inside out of the iron ore plain. Tailings bury a world of stillness, reshape a landscape of tussock grass, Spinifex rings holding the desert in place. At a slow angle man-made hills rise to meet us. Blow raw dust into a heaving sky.

Sea Cliff | MARTIN LANGFORD

A cavern of wave-slump
and suction so casual
you search
for each half-glimpse of plastic
that once had a point.

Slick water streaming
        like blood
through a carnivore's teeth.

Nowhere to start from
and nowhere to end
where the waves thud and hiss—
and the one thing they say
is *More flotsam, more chaos, more wrack.*

Sheer rock fades back—
        but you still see enough
to know every small link in your alibi—
each temperate claim—
        will be mush in these claws:

nightmare that rears without trying. . .

Like a dictator's cutie in folk-dress,
you could walk through the Gross Fugue—
or hold out a tray full of poems.

But no smear of virtuous twinkling
        will pacify this.

Last birds call out for their hollows.

Soon, you'll head back
to your warm box of rough calculations—
shut your eyes tight, and stare down:
at gleams of insouciant masses, lurching and dropping
beneath you, and slapping, all night.

sealed tight for safety | HASIB HOURANI

i call my suburb the god district
        because there's a church on every corner
        because the sunsets here are beautiful
        because of all the retirement homes

sometimes i close my eyes
crossing melville road sometimes
the signal isn't mine heel slips
into tram track heel slips out

here's where i saw god this week:
        on night-time concrete, while jumping, singing
        the wattlebird watching me write this
        my favourite cup shattering on the bathroom sink

i make dinner to Survivor
i get into bed with a nineteen year-old
scandinavian and his axe
he is building a log cabin from scratch
he is chipping at timber
he is knocking me asleep

god in my ice cream
because
that 7eleven is atop a hill
i can see the whole world
my parents tell me hello

                                      slurp
                there's that final suck
            before my window sip
                 is fully wound gulp
              and the citylink gasp
                  is a world away

            there's the fact that
                the muffle starts
before the ute hits your bonnet
                         and then there's ringing

i'd like to make a shrine
in my living room
but i can't find an altar on gumtree
and my hands have been so shaky lately
and chicken wire makes me bleed

shards of shattered blue
like sledgehammer to screen
like riverbank in sweden
            in winter and
        a strong man's foot

when the log cabin is finished
and the   door is   closed
it   will   be   airtight
it   will   be   silent

my grandmother is with white cotton now
                and with the earth
her body will nourish the dirt and that graveyard
                will become a mountain
                it will be so high
and the sunsets will be beautiful

god saves my life every time i walk the creek and don't fall in
     i would not drown
     i would be so stunned by the water
its yuckiness
that i would stay there forever

   the muffle hits before the crash
and then there's the bits on asphalt
the last time
i saw plastic shatter like that
it was a toy
i was twelve
i was in beirut
it was under a tyre

i found a frame
on facebook marketplace
      it's silver
              like my birthname
but lost its luster
              like my birthname
the frame
is for my grandmother
for the portrait of her that i love

and i saw a photo of a heron
eating a rat
in central park
the water is brown
the rat's body is perfect

mannequin
with arms and legs
click-locked in place
petrified like that and snapped
to stay that way
forever

Self-addressed | LESH KARAN
after Sylvia Plath's 'The Couriers'

The fate of a pawn on the chessboard?
It's in the colour that plays first.

Mirrored sarees from Rajasthan?
Snagged and torn. The reflection undone.

A tongue with dental consonants?
Muted. And a mutation.

The culture in the heart and gut?
Gurgles—continuously calibrating

to what's in the ambiance. A disturbance
in the wardrobe? The selves jostling

in a single dress. Skin—
Skin!—not my address.

Sestina: Pain | STUART BARNES

Bloodied knees—my mother butterflied pain.
I wheezed like Walter from *Love and Pain
and the Whole Damn Thing* in winter. Pain
grew in my limbs nightly—I flew to Spain
in trances, entrancing as Peter Pan, pain
-lessness blooming like agapanthus. I pain

-stakingly staked out horses, my father pain
-fully pulleyed gorse. At eleven I baked *pain
au chocolat, pain au levain* and *petit pain*,
sold my soul to Betty Wright's 'No Pain,
No Gain' and Betty White's golden pain
relief. T-ball was frightening as pain

-tball, puberty fiery as Tybalt, a pain
in my neck, my gut, my butt. House of Pain
jumped me, jumped around, acid house spilled from Pain
Killers' decks, *'I will come by you into Spain'*
filled God's house, enlivening pane upon pane
—I saw another heaven. It was pain

-sworthy, unearthing Gwen Harwood's 'Pain
flows through to your brush-tip and there is changed'. Pain
dipped its toes in my backbone's waters, clacked *Pain!
Pain! Pain!*, a sort of *art autre*, southwards. *Pain
perdu* wasn't lost on your mouth. ~~Champagne~~
Sparkling white jonesed the ringing light of a pain

-ting by Louise Hearman. A world fear campaign
vowed FALLEN ANGELS! DISEASE!, but in Pain

Court, Ontario we whirled, snow angels. '*Airpane
Jerry!*' sang my nephew. '*Not now—afterpain,*'
shot my sister, hanging up. You offered *pain
doré*. Lurid tourists snapped Tommy the Pain

-ted Turtle. I hurtled *tres insultos* at Spain,
but even so loved wholly, like Walter. P.A.I.N.
—Nan Goldin's—was aureate, unlike other pain
(ἄλλος + ὀδύνη), emboldened by half-skull pain.
With stillness and a mirror my pa-in
-law forked and forked his phantom limb pain.

Pain kneaded your thin-flued heart—fingers, pain
-terish, blued. Hair Payne's grey, eyes blue as Paine
Towers—paintable, you. Now who'll share my *gros pain*?

Note: 'I will come by you into Spain' is from *Romans* 15:28, 'pain flows through to your brush-tip and there is changed' from Gwen Harwood's 'Seven Philosophical Poems'.

signs from the dead | PANDA WONG

> 'I have always wondered about the left-over
> energy, the way water goes rushing down a hill
> long after the rains have stopped'
> Adrienne Rich—'For the Dead'

signs from the dead were clotting up the world's arteries. all sorts of
weird theatrical shit was happening all the time, clouds twisting into semiotic

shapes & dog excrement arranged in profound & mysterious patterns.
I was finding double yolks in every cracked egg & receiving mysterious hoax

emails about God, heaven & cryptocurrency & AI telemarketing calls asking
me… *have you recently been in a car crash?* my psoriasis was flaring up in

sexy & esoteric epidermal crop circles. what were the dead trying to
tell me? there was a very real possibility that I was coating things with a

cinematic glaze. like ancient viruses sleeping in the Antarctic's thick ice, I was
not ready to feel after feeling so much. have you ever seen a salmon cannon?

they are devices that catapult salmon across dams. a commenter on Reddit
wonders if salmon think that they are portals to another world. 2017 was the

year of realising things. 2017 was the year I was propelled into another world.
I was writing poems about grief. I was trying to milk my pain dry. I believed

that writing was a way of closing in, getting intimate with the details. I
failed to remember that moving closer to something can mean moving

further away from something else. I wrote about grief so much that
I sucked the marrow out of its meaning. semantic satiation tasted

like a used bandage, so familiar that it started to disgust me. I fracked my
feeling core until the meaty centre of my heart closed over. things became

so absurd with sadness, all logic leaked away. like this video I watched of
a mum absolutely losing it as a baby lisps its very first word… *anthwopocene.*

or like this time Ann from work gave me a handmade card after my dad died.
she had painstakingly cut out & pasted an image of a vaguely azn girl to the

front. I was confused by the racial inaccuracy & touched by the meticulous
penmanship & completely unprepared for the revelation that Ann was a devout

Mormon & this was a devout Mormon card & that she had written her devout
Mormon email inside so I could begin my devout Mormon journey!!! all I can

say is that some people see pain as a franchising opportunity. I'm thinking
about that one Joan Didion quote that people always send you, *a single person*

is missing for you and the whole world is empty, when someone you love
has died & when you would rather be left the fuck alone. the way the word

missing hisses out into the air from behind clenched teeth & how the *missing*
will stretch on & on into the rest of my life like a blaring Hummer limo with

lights ablaze. I used to think of grief as something to be purged. but now I
feel differently. I feel it multiplying in my cells   metabolising in my small

intestine   flaking off my scalp   pooling in the corners of my eyes. a new
haggard body part to add to my ongoing collection of haggard body parts.

last night, I watched a film where the sad protagonist asks his staunch driver
to take him somewhere she likes. they end up at a garbage plant watching

clumps of trash fall from the sky with a strange grace. turning to him, she
says…   *doesn't it look like snow?*

Note: This poem was also produced in collaboration with local musician Hannah Wu as a track,
which can be listened to here: https://pandawong.bandcamp.com/track/signs-from-the-dead

something specific about this boodja | NADIA RHOOK

'Something universal this way you become'
—Aditi Machado, 'Then', 2019.

I try to pause systematically before I drop you at childcare

on the way to the car we watch pearly dew slide along the leaves of a
debatably toxic shrub, the father in me wanting you to
love the leaves as much as you love risk the mother in me wanting to keep you
far away from all things remotely poisonous as if it's possible to separate
imported trees from care from trips to the children's hospital where
an Australian family are still demanding to hear why their daughter's
case was not escalated why not all bodies appear equal in this story why
not all suburbs are built from the clay that lies beneath them

tomorrow I'll find a way to explain to you why you should stay
suspicious of rules that pertain to keep planets from colliding but
ignore the way it's impossible to separate gravity from movement from breath
sweetheart there are celestial bodies there are living breathing bodies, there are bodies marked
for immediate medical attention

in the
   car I sing you twinkle twinkle en Castellano wondering if it's
      familiar to you yet taking pleasure in three minutes of deviance from
         this colony's language sure you must hear in my elastic vowels the way
           Castellano has yet to travel from my tongue through my bellybutton into the evenly
         spaced grammar of my spine sure you can
      hear that this language neither belongs to the boodja speeding beneath us

estrellita, donde estas?
quiero verte titilar

     at the traffic lights we stop

two stars
    held close to earth only by seat belts burn our specific selves
    high above the warmed clay bricks of Maylands

Songs you can't hear | TIMMAH BALL

Before silence
There were lyrics
A woman in a building
Sung histories we imagined
Still fixed to our homes[1]

Site-specific sound
Within an app
Tethered to zoom
On the Internet
Writing sites like the Mill
In an email
Physical buildings
We hadn't met[2]

Before silence
We saw words
In her mouth
About workers
In a factory that burned
Like we knew[3]

Discussing labour
You can't see
From experiences
You don't know
Hosiery and socks
Before bespoke was advertised
And handmade was new[4]

Before silence
We asked if
We still hear?
What doesn't exist?
Unsure if
Sounds change
Still fixed to our homes[5]

Purpose, specificity,
Labour, manufacturing
Just words
On the Internet
Writing songs
You can't hear[67]

[1] **On March 13** before the city *slipped* from view, I received a commission from Liquid Architecture and More Art to develop lyrics for a singer in response to the Lincoln Mills Chimney, a tall hollow brick structure behind Bunnings in Cobourg. I imagined a woman in the abandoned building singing for the factory workers who had been employed there overtime. But was unsure how to write about gentrification when the precursory terra nullius meant so much more.

[2] **On March 16** a state of emergency was declared and the Mill became a cerebral image and the concept of public art disappeared as quickly as it reappeared online. We grieved for what we imagined we'd lost even though we knew there was something bigger. Joel said that *'the chimney is such a rich context for thinking about material and immaterial conditions—being a literal echo chamber housed within bricks-and-mortar. But perhaps it could be mobilised in another way.'* So we kept pushing as Jessie acknowledged that *'it feels very secondary for me at the moment, but I think after nearly 6 years of parenting I am accustomed to having to delay things, put them on hold, put them aside etc. without panicking that they will get lost.'*

[3] **On April 6** I saw the former workers of Lincoln Mills as a continuum of the broader working class struggles that the virus accentuated. I told Joel and Jessie that *'the idea of responding to a physical factory seems incredibly powerful and strange and almost painfully ironic given the fact that artists are so often the culprits of taking over these buildings, most commonly 'the converted warehouse' and turning them into a studio/bar/gallery/performance space which become highly desirable but almost in contrast to the original work that took place. Work that was and continues to be devalued culturally and intellectually. I've also seen wonderful critiques by artists during the crisis explaining that the reason we are in this predicament is because we never developed stronger solidarity with factory workers, hospitality, casual retail, contract cleaners, etc. Instead, we saw ourselves as more important and different to those professions in our own struggles for higher wages and financial security, even though we're not and in fact interdependent given the huge number of artists who work in hospo to pay the rent.'* I later discovered that in 1925 the factory was partially burnt down and while the night watchmen were sure no workers were on the premises, something in the retelling felt uneasy like a warning or realisation that the gap between their story and those who write it was boundless and unfair.

[4] On October 5 I found out that the Lincoln Knitting and Spinning Mills was one of the largest textile manufacturers in Australia, giving employment to approximately 800 people, a large percentage women and girls. Joel, Jessie and I had a zoom meeting and we tried to link these threads, imagining what a site-specific sound installation looked like in a local government arts context within an app.

[5] On October 7 I couldn't hear any sounds from the Mill. Joel offered me a workers permit to visit the site which felt like a betrayal or a resounding privilege when I imagined the other types of workers who needed permits, whose labour seemed much more urgent but always invisible. I was just telling a story and wasn't sure if it was work. But documenting these tensions felt necessary even if the sound was unclear.

[6] On October 16 I was sent a document containing links to historical references and contemporary upgrades. The Lincoln Mills had recently been rebranded as a Homemakers Centre, as if feminised labour had reached its capitalist end point. But the sound of sabotaged knitting machinery echoed through the Centre, which included a Bunnings Warehouse, a Clive Peters store, an Officeworks, and a gym. The protests of three female workers who in 1932 interfered with motors to instigate a stop-work meeting against low wages were still audible within the new shopping complex. I tried to imagine what the workers of the future might sell in the additional 30,000m^2 of peripheral retail space still available within the precinct. Caught in a cycle of commercial potential producing goods you can't feel but relentlessly desire, would we still hear the voices of resistance within the capitalist machine?

[7] On October 29 This poem was recorded in Arabic. The translation or trans-creation resonated in multiple ways as I tried to connect the unfamiliar sounds, I heard with the words that I had written. Translating the poem into other languages to reflect migration patterns in Coburg became an important way to ground its placelessness to people in the absence of a live performance. But this gesture exposed the erasure of First Nations languages through the process of colonisation, which separated Woi Wurrung and other languages from their land. We could reach for multiple tools and resources to translate the poem into numerous languages but interpreting it into Koorie languages was complex, as the custodians of this land have and continue to be neglected. Translations between English and First Nations languages are rarely possible as English obscures the aural quality of Aboriginal languages. However, interpretation as a slow and guided relationship of repatriation is occurring. Wiradjrui academic and writer Jeanine Leanne describes in Guwayu that:

> The use of the term 'interpretation' rather than translation is a conscious choice and one recommended by participating Elders and Custodians. The term speaks more faithfully to the complexity of each of our languages that are unique and refuse direct classification and translation into the coloniser's introduced language of English.

Although this poem currently stands in the introduced language of English, we imagine that this is temporary and will change in an ongoing process of de-centring English, which cannot be rushed or moulded into Westernised methods of translation.

still the night parrot sings | JAZZ MONEY
after Dean Cross Icarus, my Son

watch the boy fall sky to dust and through
he doesn't land on that promised confetti
but instead feels the crunch
something that slips through dreams
and cannot be held in morning light
landing hard on a cold hard thing

        it sounds like a truck tearing along the highway
        seen by the country it crosses unseeing

        it looks like a cricket bat turned tired
        yelling out in boxing day backyards of almost and could have
        years gone almost and he could have been a—

    cuz, is it true
that you can move away and slip into a new skin
polish up the nasal of your accent
and find ways to never tell the full story
of the thing you will learn the name for in the city
    what is it that they say
it's only once there is a distance between yourself and poverty
that you might see that it was there all along

        maybe it lives in that back shed
        maybe it lives under those creaking floors
        and if you wait long enough in that city
        you might even begin to recall housing insecurity and a black eye
        as some sort of ridgy-didge bullshit badge of genuine
                ascendence

>   *I heard em whisper*

did you see him before the fall
two fists raised and back gleaming
a proper champion
for us eyes to gaze upon
maybe that uncle built him up wrongways inside this labyrinth
>   *but here's the thing*

I am so sick of you force feeding
those myths of elsewhere upon this soil
where we have story plenty
and it doesn't end like this

you wrote him in to fall
but I can see him rising

>   it sounds like a whistle in dawn light
>   the call of soft returning
>   it's dark out with only the headlights
>   to reveal feather and confetti falling
>   *but yes cuz, still the night parrot sings*

>   it looks like a man returning
>   adjusting the flaking ghost gum print
>   hanging proud above the laundry sink

and if you look at him just right in the city light glow of elsewhere
I can see that story true
they said falling
but I say rising
I say floating
say returning

Surfacing | MICHELLE CAHILL
at Darling Point

a vantage looking out to the Heads, where foreigners came
   penumbras of lush, canopied foliage
ficus macrophylla, ficus rubiginosa, Bangalow and kentia palms
       my phone pings with an ambivalent date,
and the ferry chugs away from the pontoon to Rose Bay

   our tongues like waves, thumping the breakwater's
imbroglio of rocks   grottos churn the dark blue, white brocade
        as if demanding an answer

a boy in yellow jacket pulling through   this chatoyant light
how it mesmerises those wrecked here on tidemarks
   come surfacing, thrumming, fade in, fade out   a pair of cormorants
      synchronise mid-flight   a flare of sense-drenched ideas
    (recall my father reading Keats   euphonious, as
water timer jet-ski helicopter   be the surveyor of paragraphs
   each an island, every line a perimeter   be the gap, not the view
      between trees, a red canoe dipping & rising
marks its manifesto,   hard sunlight on the weathered jetty poles
their oyster socks,)   we give ourselves permission for what—
     our bodies being invaded   never owned

sleep's heavy on my lids   perchance to drift, with the crushing
       tide of predictable texts,   #worklife
#writinglife #waves #poetry#poetryisnotdead

Surfing Again | SIMONE KING

For Mark

The sea calms and the surfers form a circle in the water under the late morning sun. Pat holds the Tupperware, the calcium-carbonate tailings of you. He tells your myth: the fearless traveller before Lonely Planet walking the desert palace of Leh, flinging the train doors open to the Nag Champa air and flowered corpses of Varanasi. *Enjoy, my friend*, I imagine him saying, *this next destination, this last opening of light.* I'm stranded on the tideline, toes furling and unfurling in foam. My stories are smaller—cumin seeds crushed in a mortar, curry passed between us in your succulent garden, and how, as I pushed you in your chair toward the sea to watch a rising swell, your creased face calmed. Now the red box that holds you trembles. The surfers turn and find the sea and ride the break in one bronze line. And I see how the sea makes all bodies one. Pat pulls off the lid, and all the pieces of you—the punch lines of your jokes, your love of Marquez, marijuana and strong women—return, meet their final belonging, in salt water.

Tabulations (A Nine Year) | GRACE YEE

First thing, The Morning News: Virus Travel Expedited by Cool Dry Air. We are in jade country, on a narrow path, a steep incline, in search of pounamu, which they say is more durable than steel.

All over the world, as young men of industry (action heroes) whirr above vaulted ceilings, it remains the custom to eulogize animated women with tiny glass feet and alabaster skin.

Studies have shown that people perceive odd numbers to be masculine and even numbers to be feminine. Everything begins with one, and nine's persistence and omnipresence (despite feline conclusions) is second to none, which is not to say it is second to zero.

It's 36 degrees but I am forbidden to swim in the river. Mother says the current is too cold for girls. *The Boy got to be stron*g, she says, to pick up refrigerators and car chassis. I must stay inside and keep detailed notes that correspond closely to my body parts.

The situation is competitive and the hunger harrowing, but what can I do—the sun is not mine to stare at. My job is to eat well enough to safeguard the eggs, but not so well that they can't be fertilised supine. A delicate mission.

Every spring the neighbour to the south butchers the wattle tree because the wife finds their semen-like fragrance nauseating. The neighbours to the north hurl hysterias from cranes that track my country's airspace.

On this land anxiety is a double brick house. It shelters a menagerie of writhing creatures locked in and fed after dark.

I could wait for heavy showers. I could set wider margins.

But the tabulations are not up to me. According to the terms of this contract, to notify a change of address or cancel my subscription, I must consent to the terms and conditions before contacting customer service.

Talara'tingi | FELICITY PLUNKETT

To lie among flames, to come through fire
in the shape of a star—(o hope)—

feathery. To push pink past char, woolly
across heath and open forest, clumping

to blush, jump bruised blue eucalypt
-hazed mountains lying grazed—(o hope)—

To be given a man's name—*forsythii*—not to be
named, to be nameless, to know

what it is to be spoken over, spoken
of, pressed. To open underground—(o hope)—

To come back—hailed by lyre, by whip—from
catastrophe—after the flicked

cigarette, flash of hand and stripe of dry
lightning. To follow the drowning—(o hope)—

carrying colour like a blanket. To labour in fire
'furnished with rays'—*actinotus*—homeless. To go

across razed borders under a burgeoning
enemy's thunder, after everything

To offer an artillery of fluffy seeds to breeze, open
velvety bracts high above cousins coasting

silver. To hold dew-nectar morning bright, to soothe
the wounded. To be wounded, to lie under disaster

—(o hope)—To make something anyway. To turn
from your moribund cradle into roseate light, into air—

—(o hope)—

Tenebrae | THEODORE ELL

Nightfall on the sill. Trinkets, hardened dust. Sky
in the gaps of a broken comb—the medley

of towers, antennae. The city: a queue
for dinner at a swish place, or a catwalk.

Thoughts of not doing an evening by halves—
not dress circles or crystal filled in series,

only forgetting the rule of doubt for hours,
leaving morning till morning, whole vacancies.

This sill, monogrammed by wine rims. A living.
Rest from studying the pavement in silent lines,

from the cold communion, aid. Frail-voiced
nuns chant responses from behind gilt fences

through the workless days. They reach some in the street,
who look in, down a ribcage of coloured light,

high rafters, canopy—a keyhole vision
of dusk between towers, that toothed horizon,

a light that breaks our outline, hides our numbers.

Transported | LOU GARCIA-DOLNIK

After Mirka Mora's 'Lovers Being Transported by Birds to the Land of Love' (1961)

Imagine: last night's apparition emerged as a chrysalis
from the depths of physics' imaginary calculus. Down
was up and up, the distempered gesture risen
from the errors of fever's elemental questioning.
Cosmic sheets tossed like rag dolls which have sown
themselves into likeness. Avians cantillating
against the grain of evening's everlasting nuzzle.
Birds were still birds: tonal patterns clusterfucking
the material of their exogenous ontologies. Time's measure
the echolocation of wings on air's fundamental frequencies.
From a height, the imminent earth terrain left behind,
disproving gravity's categorical imperative. Memory
an unfaithful object like so many late feet in the snow
of sempiternal winter. The coast still the coast: horizon
dissolved by metaphor's abstractions like so many doves
agitating the topsoil of lamplight's periodic waves.
The ground is territory we barely touch with our feet,
so much are our souls for allegory. And love renders
the universe unintelligible. Birds carrying their cargo
with sound for fear of descending the day's bright inquiry.
As if unknowing Icarus by the names given his anxious
Father. As if tying his blue-ribbon dovetail upward.
The endless, indolent sky. The sun's cautionary colours.

Two Cities | JARAD BRUINSTROOP

I.

Nobody in Rome cares
that I have begun
to devour you.
In the hostel this morning
and again tonight.
Even on the basilica stairs
while the nuns pray inside.

II.

Late fall is the time to begin
composing winter music—
when everything yearns
to be soft and lean.
At night the air
on the corner of Madison
and Fifty-seventh is faint
with hunger for snow.

Watching Adrianne Lenker Play Guitar with a Paintbrush
KRISTIAN RADFORD

slow-motion cool, calligraphing the air as if to polish sound
to a diamond, as if to brush your way into the core
of the simple progression, everything about you is a light
touch, a deft waltz shuttling fractals across a barn floor in
looping peregrinations, I imagine zooming in close to
the vibrations and getting lost in their gentle chaos
the muted strings humming around me like hair, I imagine
the roughness of the wind as it traffics around the sound hole
pushing waves of dusklight back into the room's lungs
a breeze whipped up by a fast body in a wide skirt
your weakstrong voice perfect and scarcely believable, your
porcelain mask brittle but whole, I haunt your desert world
as the sun wings through the open windows, a different sun
to mine, older and tired, glowing with the waxy orange of
experience, your song suspended in the atmosphere
like a wince, a smirk, the percussion of ideal love
everything temporary but falling exactly into place, then you
paint yourself and your song out of the picture until all that's left
is the dry air, the stopped breath, the shock of a heart cracking
under the weight of incomprehensible fullness

The Weight of Words | JENA WOODHOUSE

> *Back to the land of dreams and loneliness,*
> *Where **we** are highnesses and majesties—*
> —Marina Tsvetaeva

These cloisters heard the voices, once, of Gogol',
Tolstoy, Lermontov, issuing from tomes left
open in the sandstone teaching rooms; echoed
with the brittle laughter of the febrile Silver Age;

tinkle of raised champagne flutes, the poets of
Saint Petersburg, their voices clear, ephemeral
as ice; their lines a litany of lives that soon
would be curtailed, excised, snuffed out like votive

flames in garrets gnawed by fear and rage; in gulags,
or by firing squads—the fate of Hofstein, Gumilev.
This quadrangle was crowded with the stories
outlawed by the state, that slipped through apertures

in time to seek refuge, a hiding-place, where students
hungry for the taste of otherness, authentic grace,
devoured page by page the testaments of those brief,
haunted, hectic lives who'd lost their frames,

their journeys wrenched awry by unforgiving states,
but not their terms of reference, the acts of conscience,
art, and faith; who lived to write, because there seemed
no other way to be; create: because to write their truths

was to survive. They've gone, those generous
companions of our student days. The cloisters hold no
echo of their transitory ways; the students aged,
though youthful voices stay with them as word and phrase:

the specific gravity, in other tongues, of sound
and sense; the weight of language rising, falling,
travelling through time and space: words evoking
worlds internalised, with no external trace—save this

sublimated memory of prophets, saints, and knaves—
whose words we weighed, and took to heart,
and pocketed as talismans, to signify the sense
we gleaned, from Chekhov, from Akhmatova:

a quality not readily defined, yet recognised—
an art that celebrates integrity in poetry
and plays, by poets who were doomed
to die in art's embrace, but never fade—

The Wolves of Mayo | ANNE WALSH
(for my grandmother)

You kept Irish on your tongue like the last Christmas candy
you try to keep going because you can't get any more like that
You were never a local anywhere I ever saw you not since you left
Ireland so long before that your memory of it slanted like snow
under someone else's memory of a streetlamp in winter
That furious quiet that anchorite white
an electric pink prayer falling up from its face
And you never went back
I'm sure that's why I was born with a chest that's a ship of goodbye
why I've left every place I've ever lived, why *I'm* a local nowhere
Why I carry goodbye with me like a business card, like hello
Why no one can place the *where* of how I speak
because the where of what's underneath my voice
isn't from here, it's from elsewhere, the between worlds
      I write past midnight, that the roots of Alder's bridge
          Me, The *Elsewherefarer*
since all my people before me were pulled from the trees
who cradled us in swaddling leaves and in rain that meant Everything
would be well and our wells deep as our own divining
The sticks didn't matter, we were walking aquifers
we didn't have to look for water, it was us, the song
      Of stars in blanket bog and the sweet scent of turf
         fire thick as chocolate in moonlit rooms
After blown out candles and clayed slanes' wings rested by the flames,
it was no Big Bang to hold a stick that would turn for us
It was just to hold the Hazel, the hand of a lover

not to lead us to water, we were horse and felt where it was

The land we knew was a little bit of mud mixed with ocean my dreams

are still of dark seas like the mad core off Inishmore

where at night there's no horizon only a crow wing portal

between here

    And Tír

        na nÓg

We didn't come back in the morning

but we return every night by moonlight in my Clipper heart you

were nineteen when you had to leave Breaffy

and your dad's new grave and the dog by the door,

twenty-one when you married a man in Philadelphia who hit you

when he drank and he drank all the time, how the time must've dragged

    A dead limb,

        a possum shocked by cat's teeth

A fox the colour of sunset gutted by a man in a coat

who blew a horn before he hit you, made a sport of it

But there's shale colour in a fox tale, ochre seams, the geology of

listening

to stars biting into the sky of your eyelids

in the cathedral made of trees god built when she first fell

    In love was your language

        not the tick of a clock with only a big hand

sounding eternity in its hour of silence, set to the cuckoo bruises on

your arm

and to the endlessnesses of you and the kids hiding

in the closet, untimeable forevers

(my hour ghost limbs still feel safer in a closet)
You couldn't save them from him, especially poor little Joe
Did you dream then of the wolves of Mayo?
        An even older memory than yours, could you hear
                them howling in Philadelphia so far past
real midnight that Primary Night was again
and you ran in it with the wolves
and they spoke Irish
and the night sounded like a river
Did you remember then?
        Did you remember the language of yourself in All
                that blue light and lips curled off fangs
Running from a man to the wolves?
Tell me in Irish our Christmas candy language,
light my fairy tongue with choice
it seems I've made all the wrong ones, like you trusted
false loves who don't speak tree
        Now fifty
               sleeping on a friend's couch
Forge in my smithy mouth your master silver work of loss
and I will speak in our leaf language, with our alphabet of trees
and play with little Joe in all the Birches, Rowans, Alders,
Willows, Ash, Hawthorns, Oaks, Holly, Hazel, Apple, Vine,
Ivy, Reed, Blackthorn, Elder, Fir, Gorse, Heather, Poplar, Yew and Pine
        who taught us Irish, that ear singing
                their lullaby of wind
of rain, of wolves, of worlds, of no goodbyes

The Yield | EUNICE ANDRADA
after Sonia Feldman

When I read there were 170 women
seized from brothels in the Gardenia
district, loaded into police wagons
and crammed into the hull of a ship,
I wonder if they held hands. Or prayed.
If they cried when their lurching cage
docked, and when next morning
they were forced to till the dizzying
fields. I wonder how they felt
when told it was a waste
for pleasure to bear no fruit,
how they must instead keep
the earth fertile with their hands.
I wonder about the small protests:
if they slashed open the mouths
of green coconuts to drink in
the juice in croaking afternoons,
if, while wrenching cassava from
the dirt, they spat jokes about the men
who must be asking for them, if they
sang ballads under their breath
while they worked, if they made
love to each other and did not wait
for the yield.

Your Bones of Glass | DAMEN O'BRIEN

They say that in the ocean, there are creatures made of glass:
their delicate bones, brittle as a wish, their gooseflesh sensitive skin.
It may be so. The ocean is vast and mostly unexplored, as love is.
Other fish see only windows clear as the water they swim through,
or their own mirrors, tailing and turning in synchronicity, pale cyphers.
Such shardy creatures must be rare—they cannot see themselves,
they must not touch. Their love-making slow and uncertain, full of
edges, proceeding in sympathy—every word they speak might cut.
I don't think that they are lonely. I think they are cautious, considerate.
From what I have seen of the vitreous collisions of desire, it may be so.
But sometimes when we come together in the sloshy depths of dark, the
water is briefly luminous, our touch is like the chiming of bells, like the
soft celebration of two champagne glasses, full of bubbles, full of light.

Notes on Contributors

Adam Aitken was born in London, spent his early childhood in Malaysia, Thailand and Perth, before settling in Sydney. He received the Patrick White Award in 2021. *Revenants* (Giramondo) is his most recent book.

Claire Albrecht is a poet, editor and curator from Mulubinba (Newcastle) NSW. She was the 2019 Emerging Writers Festival fellow at the State Library of Victoria, a 2020 Varuna 'Writing Fire, Writing Drought' fellow, and the 2021 West Darling Arts Writer in Residence. She is a resident at the Helene Wurlitzer Foundation, New Mexico in 2022. Claire's debut chapbook *pinky swear* was published in 2018, and her most recent book *handshake* was shortlisted for the Puncher & Wattmann First Poetry Book Prize. She is Editor-in-Chief of *The Suburban Review*.

Eunice Andrada is a poet and educator. Her first poetry collection *Flood Damages* (Giramondo Publishing, 2018) won the Anne Elder Award and was a finalist for the Victorian Premier's Literary Award for Poetry and the Dame Mary Gilmore Award. Her celebrated second poetry collection *TAKE CARE* (Giramondo Publishing, 2021) has gained honours as a finalist for the Judith Wright Calanthe Award, The Stella Prize, Australian Literature Society Gold Medal and two NSW Premier's Literary Awards. Born and raised in the Philippines, she currently lives and writes on unceded Gadigal Land.

Timmah Ball is a writer and zine maker of Ballardong Noongar heritage. Her most recent zine/micro publication is *Do Planners Dream of Electric Trees?* created through Arts House Makshifts publics.

Stuart Barnes is the author of *Like to the Lark*, out February 2023 with Upswell Publishing, and *Glasshouses* (UQP, 2016), which won the 2015 Arts Queensland Thomas Shapcott Poetry Prize, was commended for the 2016 Anne Elder Award and shortlisted for the 2017 Mary Gilmore Award. His 'Sestina after B. Carlisle' won the 2021/22 Gwen Harwood Poetry Prize.

Alison J Barton is a Naarm-based poet and descendant of the Wiradjuri people. Themes of race relations, Aboriginal-Australian history, colonisation, gender and psychoanalytic theory are central to her work. She has been published in Australian and international poetry and literary journals including *Overland, Australian Poetry Journal, Otoliths, Rabbit, Westerly Mag, StylusLit, Mascara Literary Review, The Storms* (Ireland), *Poethead* (Ireland) and *The Night Heron Bark*s (USA). In 2022 Alison received a commended place in the WB Yeats Poetry Prize for Australia, was shortlisted for both the Queensland Poetry Oodgeroo Noonuccal Poetry Prize and the *Pratik Magazine Fire and Rain* edition prize, and long listed for the inaugural Liquid Amber Press Poetry Prize.

Kim Cheng Boey is the author of six collections of poetry, a travel memoir entitled *Between Stations*, and *Gull Between Heaven and Earth*—a historical novel about the Tang Dynasty poet Du Fu.

Ken Bolton cuts a moodily romantic figure within the dun Australian literary landscape. Morose, counter-intuitive, something of a zany, his name inevitably conjuring perhaps that best known image of him, bow-tie askew, grinning cheerfully, at the wheel of his 1955 Jaguar D-type, El Cid. His most recent book is *Fantastic Day*, from Puncher & Wattmann in 2022.

Peter Boyle is a Sydney-based poet and translator of poetry from Spanish and French. His ten books of poetry have won numerous awards, including the South Australian Premier's Award, the Queensland Premier's Award and the Kenneth Slessor Poetry Prize. His most recent books of poetry are *Enfolded in the Wings of a Great Darkness* (2019), *Notes Towards the Dreambook of Endings* (2021) and *Ideas of Travel* (2022). As a translator he has eight books published, including four books by Cuban poet José Kozer, *The Trees: Selected Poems of Eugenio Montejo*, and *Jasmine* for Clementina Médici by Uruguayan poet Marosa di Giorgio. In 2013 he was awarded the New South Wales Premier's Award for Literary Translation.

David Brooks lives in the Blue Mountains. His latest book is *Turin: Approaching Animals* (meditations, 2022). His most recent collection of poetry is *Open House* (UQP, 2016). He is currently working on a *New and Selected Poems* (UQP, 2024).

Jarad Bruinstroop's debut poetry collection won the 2022 Thomas Shapcott Poetry Prize and is forthcoming from UQP in 2023. He is the 2022 UQ Fryer Library Creative Writing Fellow. He holds a PhD in Creative writing from QUT where he also teaches.

joanne burns is a Sydney poet. Her latest poetry collection *apparently* was published by Giramondo Publishing in 2019. She is currently assembling a new collection *rummage*.

Michelle Cahill is a Sydney poet and novelist of Indian heritage. Her short story collection *Letter to Pessoa* won the NSW Premier's Literary Award for New Writing. *Daisy and Woolf* was recently published by Hachette. Her awards include the Hilary Mantel International Short Story Prize, a Fellowship at Hawthornden Castle, the Arts Queensland Val Vallis Award and the Red Room Australian Poetry Fellowship. She has been twice shortlisted in the Helen Anne Bell Bequest and her poems have appeared in *Meanjin*, *Southerly* and *Poetry Island Review*.

Bonny Cassidy is a settler of Irish and German descent, living in Dja Dja Wurrung forest outside Castlemaine. She is the author of three poetry collections, most recently, *Chatelaine* (Giramondo Publishing, 2017) which was shortlisted for the Prime Minister's Literary Awards 2018. Her first book of nonfiction, ~~Monument~~ is forthcoming in 2023. With Jessica L Wilkinson, Bonny co-edited the anthology, *Contemporary Australian Feminist Poetry* (Hunter Publishers, 2016). She teaches creative writing at RMIT University, Melbourne.

Derek Chan holds a First-Class Honours in Literary Studies from Monash University, where he received the Arthur Brown Thesis Prize. His writing has appeared in journals and anthologies such as *Best of Australian Poems, Australian Poetry Anthology, Cordite Poetry Review, Meanjin, The Margins, Juked* and elsewhere. He has been a finalist for awards by Frontier Poetry and Palette Poetry. He is currently an MFA candidate at Cornell University, where he is an editorial associate for *EPOCH* and a university fellow.

Nandi Chinna's most recent collection *The Future Keepers* was shortlisted for the Prime Minister's Literary Award in 2020 and was highly commended in the Victorian Premier's Prize 2019. Nandi was recently granted the 2021 Western Australian Premier's Fellowship.

Eileen Chong is a poet and the author of nine books. Her most recent collection is *A Thousand Crimson Blooms* (UQP, 2021). She lives and works on unceded Gadigal land.

Emilie Collyer lives on Wurundjeri land where she writes across and between poetry, prose and performance. Her work is published and produced widely. Her debut full-length poetry collection is published in 2022 by Vagabond Press: *Do you have anything less domestic?* Emilie is a current PhD candidate at RMIT where she is researching feminist creative practice.

Angela Costi is the author of five poetry gatherings/books including *Honey & Salt* (Five Islands Press, shortlisted Mary Gilmore Prize 2008) and *An Embroidery of Old Maps and New* (Spinifex, 2021). Also, nine produced plays/performance-text (five commissioned and funded). Her poetry has placed/shortlisted in a number of prizes including Woorilla, Meniscus and joanne burns Microlit Awards. Since 1994, she's been published widely in Australia and overseas. In 2021, she received the High Commendation for Contribution to Arts and Culture, Merri-bek Award. She is known as Αγγελικη Κωστη among the Cypriot diaspora, which is her heritage. She lives on Wurundjeri Woi Wurrung land.

Louise Crisp is the author of *Yuiquimbiang* (Cordite, 2019), shortlisted for the 2020 Victorian Premier's Literary Awards. Her latest collection is *Glide* (Puncher & Wattmann, 2021). 'Leafless–Leafs' was written as part of Stony Creek Collective a multi-artform project in the foothill forests of East Gippsland (Gunaikurnai country). The project was supported by the Victorian Government through Creative Victoria.

Judith Crispin is a poet and visual artist with ancestry from the Bangerang people of the Murray River, as well as from Scotland, France, Mali, Senegal and the Ivory Coast. She has published two collections of poems, *The Myrrh-Bearers* (Puncher & Wattmann) and *The Lumen Seed* (Daylight Books). She was the winner of the 2020 Blake Poetry Prize and her poems are regularly published in anthologies and journals. Judith lives and works on unceded Yuin Country in the Southern Tablelands, with her family and her mongrel dingo Moon.

Sarah Day's ninth book, *Slack Tide* was published in September 2022 with Pitt Street Poetry. Before that, *Tempo* and *Towards Light* (Puncher & Wattmann) were shortlisted for the Prime Minister's and Tasmanian Premier's Awards. She gratefully acknowledges the support of the 2021 Cecilie Anne Sloane Research Scholarship in writing 'Penstock Lagoon'.

Tricia Dearborn is an award-winning poet, writer and editor. Her latest books are *Autobiochemistry* (UWAP, 2019) and *She Reconsiders Life on the Run* (International Poetry Studies Institute Chapbooks, 2019). Her work is widely represented in anthologies, including *Fishing for Lightning: The Spark of Poetry*, *The Anthology of Australian Prose Poetry* and *Contemporary Australian Poetry*. She has been a guest poetry editor for literary journals including *Rabbit 31: The Science Issue* (2020), and was a judge of the 2019 University of Canberra Vice-Chancellor's International Poetry Prize. Tricia also writes fiction, and won the 2021 Neilma Sidney Short Story Prize. She is currently completing a new poetry collection with the support of a Create NSW grant.

Cath Drake is from Perth, and now lives in London, UK. *The Shaking City* (Seren Books, 2020), highly commended in the UK Forward Prize and longlisted in international Laurel Prize, followed *Sleeping with Rivers*, a Poetry Book Society choice and winner of the Seren/Mslexia pamphlet prize. Published widely in anthologies and literary journals in UK, Ireland, US and Australia, she's been short-listed for the Venture, Bridport and Manchester Poetry Prize, plus second and commended in the UK Poetry School Ginkgo eco-poetry prize. A mindfulness teacher and an award-winning environmental journalist and nonfiction writer, Cath hosts *The Verandah*, quality online poetry events for Aussie and UK writers.

Jonathan Dunk is the co-editor of *Overland* and a widely published writer. He has received the AD Hope prize and the Dal Stivens award, lectures at Deakin University and lives on Wurundjeri country.

Theodore Ell's first poetry collection, *Beginning in Sight*, was published in July 2022. 'Tenebrae' appeared in that collection and in the *Australian Book Review*. Theodore won the 2021 Calibre Essay Prize for his account of surviving the Beirut port explosion. His poetry, essays and translations have been published in Australia, the UK, Italy and Lebanon. He lives in Canberra and is an Honorary Lecturer in literature at the ANU.

Anne Elvey is a poet and researcher, living on unceded Boon Wurrung Country in Seaford, Victoria. Her recent poetry collections are *Leaf* (Liquid Amber Press, 2022) and *Obligations of Voice* (RWP, 2021). Anne is an Adjunct Research Fellow in the School of Languages, Literatures, Cultures and Linguistics, Monash University.

Brook Emery has published six books of poetry, the most recent being *Sea Scale: New and Selected Poems* (Puncher & Wattmann, 2022). He has won the Judith Wright Calanthe Prize at the Queensland Premier's Literary Awards and been shortlisted three times for the Kenneth Slessor Prize at the NSW Premier's Literary Awards.

Michael Farrell grew up in Bombala, NSW, and has lived in Melbourne since 1990. Recent book publications include *Googlecholia* and *Family Trees* (both with Giramondo). Michael's revised PhD (from the University of Melbourne) was published as *Writing Australian Unsettlement: Modes of Poetic Invention 1796–1945* (Palgrave Macmillan).

Dakota Feirer is a Bundjalung and Gumbaynggirr man and is an emergent storyteller threading his voice through innovative and interdisciplinary mediums. His work has been published in *Overland Literary Journal, Wonderground Journal, Rabbit Journal, SoftStir* and *10Men Magazine*. As well as performing for live audiences including Yours and Owls Festival, the Museum of Contemporary Art and Sydney Opera House. Dakota's work consists of poems, stories and reflections that critically engage with manhood, Country, spirit and trauma; all of which informed his recent thesis which explored Indigenous cultural sovereignty. Dakota believes in healing Country and communities through art and storytelling.

Luke Fischer is a poet and philosopher. His books include the poetry collections *A Gamble for my Daughter* (Vagabond Press, 2022), *A Personal History of Vision* (UWAP, 2017) and Paths of Flight (Black Pepper, 2013), the monograph *The Poet as Phenomenologist: Rilke and the 'New Poems'* (Bloomsbury, 2015), and the co-edited volumes *Rilke's 'Sonnets to Orpheus': Philosophical and Critical Perspectives* (Oxford University Press, 2019) and *The Seasons: Philosophical, Literary, and Environmental Perspectives* (SUNY Press, 2021). He holds a PhD from the University of Sydney where he is also an honorary associate of the philosophy department.

Toby Fitch is poetry editor of *Overland* and a lecturer in creative writing at the University of Sydney. He is the author of seven books of poetry, including *Where Only the Sky had Hung Before* and, most recently, *Sydney Spleen* (Giramondo, 2021). His next book, a newly expanded and full-colour edition of *Object Permanence: Calligrammes*, will be published by Puncher & Wattmann and Thorny Devil Press alongside a solo exhibition of his visual poems at WordXImage in December 2022.

Lionel Fogarty was born on Wakka Wakka land, at Cherbourg Aboriginal Reserve in south-east Queensland in 1957. Throughout the 1970s he worked as an activist for Aboriginal Land Rights, and in the 1990s, after the death of his brother Daniel Yock, protesting against Aboriginal Deaths in Custody. His poetry collections date from the early 1980s; *Harvest Lingo* is his fourteenth collection.

Es Foong is a poet, flash fictionista and spoken word performer living on the land of the Wurundjeri people. Their poems have appeared in *Australian Poetry Journal, Rabbit Poetry, Kalliope X,* Melbourne Spoken Word's audio journal 'Audacious 4' and various anthologies, and they were shortlisted in the Liquid Amber 2022 Poetry Prize. Their debut poetry collection, *Clot* and *Marrow* is forthcoming from Recent Work Press in late 2023.

Gavin Yuan Gao (they/them) is a genderqueer immigrant poet and translator. Their debut poetry collection, *At the Altar of Touch*, was published by the University of Queensland Press in February 2022 and shortlisted for the 2022 Judith Wright Calanthe Award at the Queensland Literary Awards. They're currently a James A. Michener Fellow in the Michener Center for Writers at The University of Texas at Austin.

Lou Garcia-Dolnik is a poet of Ilocano descent working on sovereign Gadigal land. Their writing has been awarded Second Prize in *Overland*'s Judith Wright Poetry Prize, an Academy of American Poets University Prize from the University of Texas at Austin and has been shortlisted in the Blake Poetry Prize, the Arts Queensland Val Vallis Award and The LIMINAL and Pantera Press Nonfiction Prize.

Dr. Chelinay Gates aka Malardy Mulardy is an Indigenous Artist, Author, Playwright, Poet, Hypnotist, Doctor of Traditional Chinese Medicine and Mother. Chelinay the storyteller explores different genres to express the human condition. Her writing like her paintings have a dreamlike mystical quality. Using light and darkness she creates unforgettable impressions of characters and place. Such imagery is inspired by her Karajarri-Kurdish heritage and experiences living in Australia, UK, PNG, India and Singapore. Dedicated to community service and social justice, she's worked alongside Ken Colbung, Sir Ronald Wilson and Sir Frances Burt. Her first novel *Lucky-Child: The Secret* was well received by the Next Generation Indi Book Awards winning the Grand Prize for Fiction and The Best Novel over 90,000 words and in Action and Adventure. She's presently writing the sequel *The Sacred*. During the last two years she has written five plays, four under the auspices of Yirra Yaakin. This year she wrote, performed and directed a play for Short and Sweet called *Diamonds in the Dust* based around the tragic burning of her husband. Later she wrote and recorded with a cast of five a conservation themed radio play called *Caved In*. Excerpts were aired on the ABC Radio. Poetry has been a powerful way for her to express her views on Indigenous history and stories. Locally in a group called Artists and Poets Speak and internationally with her poem 'Santalum Spicatum' published in Prof. Monica Gagliano's wonderful book *The Mind of Plants*.

Stephen Gilfedder was born in Melbourne in 1948. After secondary schooling in England, he studied at the Australian National University and the University of Melbourne. He has worked variously as a mail sorter, storeman, travelling salesman, journalist, public servant, Ministerial private secretary, as media, public relations and marketing managers, advertising executive and government relations consultant. Since 1970, he has published widely in literary journals, periodicals, newspapers and anthologies of new and prize verse. His collection *Way Stations*, featuring selected verse from more than forty years, was published by Recent Work Press in 2021.

Elena Gomez is the author of *Admit the Joyous Passion of Revolt*, *Body of Work* and several pamphlets and chapbooks.

Rory Green is a writer, editor and digital media artist living on unceded Wangal land. Their debut chapbook *the attentions* was published in 2022 by Puncher & Wattmann's Slow Loris imprint. They are co-editor of digital literature journal *Crawlspace*, and Games Literature Editor for *Cordite Poetry Review*. Rory's goal is to write a poem for every Pokémon.

Jennifer Harrison has published eight poetry collections, most recently *Anywhy* (Black Pepper, 2018). She has received the Christopher Brennan Award for sustained contribution to Australian poetry and is currently chair of the World Psychiatry Association's Section for Art and Psychiatry. Her new collection *Sideshow History* will appear from Black Pepper in 2022.

Dimitra Harvey was born in Sydney to a Greek mother and grew up on Wangal country. She is the author of the chapbook *A Fistful of Hail* (Vagabond Press, 2018). Her writing has appeared in *Southerly, Meanjin, Cordite, Mascara Literary Review, SBS Voices*, and anthologies such as *The Best Australian Poems* and *The Stars Like Sand: Australian Speculative Poetry*. She was awarded third place in the 2019 Newcastle Poetry Prize for her poem 'Triptych', and won Queensland Poetry's 2021 Val Vallis Award for her poem 'Cicadas'.

Kirwan Henry is a teacher living in Perth with her husband and two children. She is reacquainting herself with her love of writing after letting life get in the way for far too long.

Barry Hill is an acclaimed writer in several genres, having won Premiers' Awards for poetry, the essay, and non-fiction. His recent books include the poems *Cold Mountain and the Sea*, and his collection of poetry reviews, *Eggs For Keeps* and the wide ranging essays, *Reason and Lovelessness*. He is possibly best known for his magnum opus, *Broken Song: TGH Strehlow and Aboriginal Possession* (2002), an excursion into Australian poetics, and *Peacemongers* (2014) his study of Rabindranath Tagore's pacifist internationalism. Having worked as a journalist and a psychologist in Melbourne and London, he has been writing full-time since 1976, when he moved to live on the Victorian coast. He has been a Post-Doctoral Fellow at the University of Melbourne, and between 1998 and 2008 was Poetry Editor for *The Australian*. *On Not Cutting Through* is the working title of a forthcoming collection that has arisen since the US flight from Kabul and the Russian invasion of Ukraine.

Maya Hodge is a Lardil and Yangkaal emerging writer, curator and creative based on the lands of the Kulin Nation. Her poetry has been published by Hardie Grant, *Cordite Poetry Review* and *Overland*. Last year, Hodge was selected as a runner-up for the SBS Emerging Writers Competition.

Sarah Holland-Batt is the author of three books of poetry—most recently *The Jaguar*—and a book of essays.

Hasib Hourani is a Lebanese-Palestinian writer, editor and educator currently living on unceded Wurundjeri Country. His practice disrupts expectations of place, archive and the relationship between the two. Through writing, he enacts processes of sprawling, fragmenting, and stitching back together. He is a 2020 recipient of The Wheeler Centre's Next Chapter Scheme and his 2021 essay, 'when we blink', was shortlisted for The LIMINAL & Pantera Press Nonfiction prize and is published in their 2022 anthology, *Against Disappearance*. Hasib is currently completing his debut publication, a book of experimental poetry about suffocation and the occupation of Palestine—excerpts of which have been published in *Australian Poetry* and *Cordite Poetry Review*. In the meantime, you can find his work in *Meanjin*, *Overland*, *Australian Poetry* and *Going Down Swinging*, among others.

Andy Jackson was awarded the inaugural Writing the Future of Health Fellowship. He lives on Dja Dja Wurrung country and his latest poetry collection is *Human Looking*, which won the 2022 ALS Gold Medal.

A Frances Johnson is an award-winning poet and artist. Her fourth poetry collection *Save As* was published by Puncher & Wattmann in 2021. *Rendition for Harp and Kalashnikov* (Puncher & Wattmann, 2017), was shortlisted in the 2018 Melbourne Prize for Literature Best New Writing Award. Previous works include the novel *Eugene's Falls* (Arcadia, 2007), which retraces the journeys of colonial painter Eugene von Guérard. Her poem 'My Father's Thesaurus' won the 2020 International Peter Porter Poetry Prize. She teaches Creative Writing at the University of Melbourne.

Jill Jones was born in Sydney and has lived in Adelaide since 2008. Her latest book is *Acrobat Music: New and Selected Poems*, published in late 2022. Recent books include *Wild Curious Air*, winner of the 2021 Wesley Michel Wright Prize, *A History Of What I'll Become*, shortlisted for the 2021 Kenneth Slessor Award and the 2022 John Bray Award, and *Viva the Real*, shortlisted for the 2019 Prime Minister's Literary Award for Poetry and the 2020 John Bray Award. In 2015 she won the Victorian Premier's Prize for Poetry for *The Beautiful Anxiety*. Her work is widely published in Australia and internationally and has been translated into a number of languages, including Chinese, French, Italian, Czech, Macedonian and Spanish. She currently writes and teaches freelance, and previously has worked as an academic, arts administrator, journalist and book editor.

Lesh Karan was born in Fiji, has Indian genes and lives in Melbourne. Her work has been published in *Australian Poetry Journal*, *Cordite Poetry Review*, *Island*, *Mascara Literary Review*, *Portside Review* and *Rabbit*, among others. Her poem 'Tense' is in the anthology *Admissions: Voices within Mental Health*. Lesh is currently undertaking a Master of Creative Writing, Publishing and Editing at the University of Melbourne.

Simone King is a poet and editor living on Wurundjeri country, Naarm/Melbourne. Simone's poems and reviews have been published in *Rabbit, Cordite, Plumwood Mountain, Right Now, Mascara Literary Review*'s *Resilience Anthology* and several poetry anthologies. Simone was awarded the 2022 Blake Poetry Prize and the 2021 Woorilla Poetry Prize, among other poetry prizes. Simone coedited *What We Carry: Poetry on Childbearing* (Recent Work Press, 2021).

John Kinsella's most recent books of poetry include *Supervivid Depastoralism* (Vagabond, 2021) and the first volume of his collected poems: *The Ascension of Sheep* (UWAP, 2022). *ART* co-written with Charmaine Papertalk Green is due out late 2022 with Magabala. He is Emeritus Professor of Literature and Environment at Curtin University.

Yeena Kirkbright is a Wiradjuri poet who grew up in Central West New South Wales. She is now blessed to live and work on Dharug and Gadigal lands in Sydney. Her work has appeared in several literary journals.

Andy Kissane lives in Sydney and writes poetry and fiction. He was joint winner of ABR's 2019 Peter Porter Prize for Poetry. *Radiance* was shortlisted for the Victorian and Western Australian Premier's Prizes and the Adelaide Festival Awards. His latest book is *The Tomb of the Unknown Artist*.

Louis Klee is a writer of poetry and philosophy. His poetry has been published widely in venues such as the *Times Literary Supplement*, the *PN Review* and the *Australian Book Review*. He won the Peter Porter Prize for his poem 'Sentence to Lilacs'.

Kristen Lang lives in mountainous country in Lutruwita / Tasmania and is working on ways to use poetry as part of a cultural response to the Anthropocene. *Earth Dwellers*, published by Giramondo in 2021, was one of 20 books longlisted for the international Laurel Prize. *SkinNotes* (Walleah Press) and *The Weight of Light* (Five Islands Press) were published in 2017.

Martin Langford is the author of eight poetry books, the most recent of which is *The Boy from the War Veteran's Home* (2022), published by Puncher & Wattmann.

Debbie Lim's poems have appeared regularly in the *Best Australian Poems* series and in *Contemporary Asian Australian Poets*, among numerous other anthologies and journals. She received the 2022 Bruce Dawe National Poetry Prize. 'Hummingbird Country' was shortlisted in the 2022 Peter Porter Poetry Prize. Her chapbook is *Beastly Eye* (Vagabond Press), and she is completing a full-length collection. She was born in Sydney, where she lives on Darramuragal land.

Caitlin Maling is a WA poet with four books of poetry, the most recent of which is *Fish Work* with UWAP (2021). A fifth book *Spore or Seed* is due out in 2023 with Fremantle Press.

Jennifer Kemarre Martiniello OAM is an award winning multidisciplinary artist of Australian Aboriginal (Lower Southern Arrernte), Chinese and Anglo-Celtic descent. As an internationally recognized glass artist her works are held in major private and public collections in Australia, the UK, USA, the Middle East, Asia and the Pacific. She received Canberra Critics Awards for both Literature and Visual Arts and received a Creative Arts Fellowship (Literature) from artsACT in 2002. Her awards include the Banjo Paterson Prize for Poetry and the Henry Lawson Short Story Prize. Her poetry, short stories and essays have been widely published in journals and anthologies in Australia and overseas, including in the *Macquarie PEN Anthology of Australian Literature, Borderless: A Transnational Anthology of Feminist Poetry* and *Not Very Quiet*. She has judged both the NSW and Queensland Premier's Literary Awards, including the David Unaipon Award for Indigenous Literature, and represented Australia as a First Nations Australian writer at the Festival of Pacific Arts in Palau 2004 and the Solomon Islands in 2012.

Glenn McPherson is a Sydney based poet and teacher. Glenn has been published in: *ACU Poetry Competition Anthology 2021/22, Finalist Anthology Newcastle Poetry Prize 2022, Liquid Amber Poetry Anthology 2022, Anthology of University of Canberra VC International Poetry Prize 2017/18, Meanjin, Southerly, Quadrant, Cordite, InDaily* (Poets Corner) and *Stilts Poetry Journal*.

Suzi Mezei is a Sri Lankan born Australian writer. She lives on Kulin land. Her writing is influenced by her cultural background, her sense of place and experience. Her work appears in journals, anthologies and collections such as *Cordite, Burrow, The Amphibian* and *Aniko*. She received the 2022 Mayor's Short Story Writing Award, is runner up in The Power of Words Prize and is the past recipient of the Ada Cambridge Writing Award for both poetry and biography. She is currently researching while in the company of clever dogs and appealing humans.

Scott-Patrick Mitchell is a queer non-binary poet who lives in Boorloo, Western Australia. Their first full-length poetry collection, *Clean*, was published by Upswell in 2022. This collection explores Mitchell's lived experience of addiction and recovery. They are also the recipient of the 2022 Red Room Poetry Fellowship plus *Westerly*'s 2022 Mid-Career Fellowship.

Audrey Molloy's debut collection, *The Important Things* (Gallery Press, 2021), won the 2021 Anne Elder Award. She collaborated with Anthony Lawrence on *Ordinary Time* (Pitt Street Poetry, 2022). Audrey was shortlisted for the 2022 Red Room Fellowship, and received a Varuna Residential Fellowship in 2020. Her work has appeared in *Meanjin, Cordite, Overland, Island, APJ* and *Southerly*. She has an MA in Creative Writing from the Manchester Writing School at Manchester Metropolitan University.

Jazz Money is a Wiradjuri poet and artist producing works that encompass installation, digital, film and print. Jazz's first poetry collection, the best-selling *how to make a basket* (UQP, 2021) was the 2020 winner of the David Unaipon Award.

Nicole Jia Moore is an Australian writer, researcher and psychology tutor at the University of Melbourne. Her poetry and non-fic has appeared in *Meanjin*, *Rabbit*, and *Cordite Poetry Review* among others.

Marjon Mossammaparast's second volume of poetry, *And to Ecstasy*, was released in March 2022 through Upswell Publishing. Her first collection, *That Sight* (Cordite Books) won the 2019 Mary Gilmore Award, was shortlisted for the 2019 Queensland Literary Awards and commended in the 2018 Anne Elder Award. Marjon was a recipient of the Neilma Sidney Literary Travel Fund in 2021. She lives in Melbourne and is a practising English teacher.

Omar Musa is a Bornean-Australian author, visual artist and poet from Queanbeyan, Australia. He has released four poetry books (including *Killernova*), four hip-hop records, and received a standing ovation at TEDx Sydney at the Sydney Opera House. His debut novel, *Here Come the Dogs*, was long-listed for the International Dublin Literary Award and Miles Franklin Award and he was named one of the Sydney Morning Herald's Young Novelists of the Year in 2015. His one-man play, *Since Ali Died*, won Best Cabaret Show at the Sydney Theatre Awards in 2018. He has had several solo exhibitions of his woodcut prints.

Damen O'Brien is a multi-award-winning poet based in Brisbane. Damen recently won the Hungry Hill Writing Poets Meets Politics competition, received Second Prize in the Bridport Poetry Competition and was shortlisted twice in the Montreal Poetry Competition. Damen's first book of poetry, *Animals with Human Voices*, was published in 2021 through Recent Work Press.

Thuy On is a critic, editor and poet. She's currently the Reviews Editor and a writer for online publication *ArtsHub*. Her first collection of poetry, *Turbulence*, was published in 2020 by UWAP. Her second, *Decadence*, was published in 2022, also by UWAP.

Reneé Pettitt-Schipp is the author of the multi-award-winning collection of poetry, *The Sky Runs Right Through Us*, written about her time teaching asylum seekers in the Indian Ocean Territories. Reneé's nonfiction work about living on Christmas Island will be released by Fremantle Press in 2023. Reneé currently lives in the Great Southern region of Western Australia.

Felicity Plunkett is a poet, critic and editor. Her most recent book is *A Kinder Sea* (UQP) and her latest essay is 'Plath Traps', published by *Sydney Review of Books*.

Claire Potter is author of four poetry collections, *Acanthus* (Giramondo), *Swallow* (Five Islands), *In Front of a Comma* (Poets Union), and *N'ombre* (Vagabond). Her poetry has been widely anthologised and published.

Kristian Radford lives in Melbourne and works as a secondary school teacher. His poetry and fiction have been published in *Meanjin, Westerly, Rabbit, Cordite Poetry Review* and other journals.

Harry Reid is a poet and co-director of *Sick Leave*. He is the author of *Leave Me Alone* (Cordite, 2022) and *the best way to destroy an enemy is to make him a friend* (Puncher & Wattmann, 2020).

Nadia Rhook is a white settler poet, historian and educator, born in Naarm and currently living in Boorloo. Her poetry appears in various journals and anthologies including *Cordite, Peril Magazine, Mascara Literary Review, Westerly* and *What We Carry: Poetry on Childbearing* (Recent Work Press). Nadia's first collection, *boots* (UWA Publishing, 2020), was released weeks before she became a pandemic mother. Her second collection, *Second Fleet Baby*, was released by Fremantle Press in 2022.

Dr. Samah Sabawi is an award-winning writer and scholar. Her critically acclaimed theatre credits include *Tales of a City by the Sea* (Currency Press, 2016) winner of two Victoria Drama awards for Best Production and Best Publication and *THEM* (Currency Press, 2021) winner of the Green Room Award for Best Writing and shortlisted for the Victorian Premier's Literary Awards and the NSW Premier's Literary Awards' Nick Enright Prize for Playwriting. Sabawi's plays were selected for the Victorian Curriculum of Education drama playlists and published by Currency Press. Sabawi co-edited *Double Exposure: Plays of the Jewish and Palestinian Diasporas* (Playwrights Canada Press, 2017), winner of Patrick O'Neill Award and co-authored *I Remember My Name: Poetry by Samah Sabawi, Ramzy Baroud and Jehan Bseiso*, (Novum, 2016) winner of Palestine Book Award. Sabawi received a PhD from Victoria University for her thesis titled *Inheriting Exile, transgenerational trauma and the Palestinian Australian Identity*.

Sara M Saleh is a human rights lawyer, community organiser, writer and the daughter of migrants from Palestine, Egypt, and Lebanon, living on Gadigal land. Her poems and short stories have been published in English and Arabic in various national and international outlets and anthologies including *Australian Poetry Journal, Cordite Poetry Review, Kill your Darlings, Meanjin, Overland Journal* and *Rabbit Poetry*. She is co-editor of the groundbreaking 2019 anthology *Arab, Australian, Other: Stories on Race and Identity*. Sara is the first and only poet to win both the Australian Book Review's 2021 Peter Porter Poetry Prize and the Overland Judith Wright Poetry Prize 2020. She is currently developing her debut novel, *Songs for the Dead and the Living* (Affirm Press, 2023) and a full-length poetry collection, *The Flirtation of Girls/Ghazl al-Banat* (UQP, 2023).

Asiel Adán Sánchez is a non-binary writer based in Naarm/Melbourne. Born and raised in Mexico, their work explores the intricacies of race, culture, gender and sexuality. Their first poetry collection, *m//otherland*, is published through Revarena Ediciones and was highly commended for the Victorian Premier's Literary Awards and The International Latino Book Awards.

Mykaela Saunders is a Koori/Goori and Lebanese writer and teacher, and the editor of *This All Come Back Now*, the world's first anthology of Blackfella speculative fiction (UQP, 2022). Mykaela won the 2022 David Unaipon Award for her manuscript *Always Will Be: Stories of Goori Sovereignty from the Future(s) of the Tweed*, forthcoming with UQP in 2023. Her novel *Last Rites of Spring* was also shortlisted for the Unaipon Award in 2020, and received a Next Chapter Fellowship in 2021. Mykaela has also won prizes for short fiction, poetry, life writing and research, including the Elizabeth Jolley Short Story Prize and the Oodgeroo Noonuccal Indigenous Poetry Prize.

Brenda Saunders is a Wiradjuri writer and artist. She has written two poetry chapbooks and three collections, including her most recent, *Inland Sea*, published in 2021 by Ginninderra Press. Her poems and reviews appear regularly in anthologies and journals both online and in print. Brenda won the 2014 Scanlon Book Prize (Australian Poetry) and in 2018, the Oodgeroo Noonuccal Prize (Queensland Poetry) and the Joanne Burns Award (Spineless Wonders). Several of her prose poems and micro fiction have been developed into prize-winning short films (Voices of Women, 2021) and recorded for 'Sonic City: Stories and Sounds of Sydney' (Spineless Wonders, 2022).

Leni Shilton is a poet and educator. She grew up in Papua New Guinea and Melbourne, and lives in Mparntwe | Alice Springs. She has written two verse novels: *Malcolm: a story in verse* (UWAP, 2019) and *Walking with Camels: The Story of Bertha Strehlow* (UWAP, 2018), the winner of the 2020 Chief Ministers Fiction Book Award. Her writing regularly appears in anthologies and journals in Australia and internationally. In 2022 she won the Inaugural Born Writers Award for her poetry collection *Voices*.

Alex Skovron is the author of seven collections of poetry, a prose novella and a book of short stories. His most recent collection is *Letters from the Periphery*, published in 2021; his earlier volume of new and selected poems, *Towards the Equator* (2014), was shortlisted in the Prime Minister's Literary Awards. Alex's poetry has appeared widely in Australia and overseas, and he has received a number of major awards for his work. *The Man who Took to his Bed* (2017), a collection of short stories, and his novella *The Poet* (2005), have been published in Czech translations; *The Attic*, a selection of his poetry translated into French, was published in 2013, and a volume of Chinese translations, *Water Music*, in 2017. His work has also appeared in Dutch, Macedonian, Polish and Spanish. The numerous public readings he has given have included appearances in China, Serbia, India, Ireland, Macedonia, Portugal and on Norfolk Island.

Yasmin Smith is a poet of South Sea Islander, Northern Cheyenne, Kabi Kabi and English heritage born on Darumbal country. She is currently an editor at University of Queensland Press (UQP) who lives on unceded Turrbal and Yuggera land.

David Stavanger is a poet, cultural producer, editor, and lapsed psychologist living on unceded Dharawal land. Co-editor of *Solid Air: Collected Australian & New Zealand Spoken Word* (UQP, 2019) and *Admissions: Voices Within Mental Health* (Upswell Publishing, 2022). David's latest collection, *Case Notes* (UWAP, 2020), won the 2021 Victorian Premier's Literary Award for Poetry.

Josie Jocelyn Suzanne is a writer/translator living on unceded wurundjeri land in Naarm. Their work has appeared in various journals, such as *Overland*, *Meanjin* and *The Suburban Review*. They are one of the recipients of the 2022 Next Chapter Fellowship, as well as the 2021 Harri Jones memorial prize and the Ultimo prize for poetry. They are a genderqueer transfemme.

Isi Unikowski is a Canberran poet, who has been widely published in Australia and overseas. His first collection, *Kintsugi*, was published in August 2022 by Puncher & Wattmann, New South Wales.

Ellen van Neerven is a writer of Mununjali and Dutch heritage born in Brisbane in 1990. Their books include *Throat*, *Comfort Food* and *Heat and Light*.

Dr. Saba Vasefi is a multi-award-winning scholar-journalist, poet and documentary filmmaker. She teaches at the University of Sydney and Macquarie University. Her report on the gendered harms of detention won the Premier's Multicultural Communications Awards. She is the editor of Red Room Poetry's Writing in Resistance. She was twice a judge for the Dolatabadi Book Prize for the Best Book on Women's Literature and Women's Issues and the BR4R Seeking Asylum Poetry Prize. She is a member of The UK Women in Refugee Law (WiRL) network and an honorary member of The Independent Scholars Association of Australia.

Ann Vickery teaches Writing and Literature at Deakin University. She is the author of three poetry collections, the most recent being *Bees Do Bother: An Antagonist's Care Pack* (Vagabond Press, 2021).

Anne Walsh is a poet and a story writer. She has been shortlisted twice for both the Newcastle Poetry Prize and the ACU Prize for literature. Her work has been widely published in print and online in Australia and in the U.S. Her two poetry collections are *I Love Like a Drunk Does* published by Ginninderra Press in 2009, and *Intact* published by Flying Islands Books in 2017. Recently, at the invitation of American actor Tituss Burgess, she read her work as part of Carnegie Hall's inaugural live online concert.

Samuel Wagan Watson is an award-winning Indigenous poet and professional raconteur. Born in Brisbane in 1972, he is of Munanjali, Birri Gubba, German and Irish descent. Samuel's first collection of poems won the 1999 David Unaipon Award. His fourth collection, *Smoke Encrypted Whispers* won the 2005 NSW Premier's Award for the Book of the Year and the Kenneth Slessor poetry prize. In 2018, Samuel was the recipient of The Patrick White Literary Award for his significant contribution to Australian literature.

Mitchell Welch, originally from Brisbane, currently resides on the Gold Coast, having spent the last decade living in Melbourne where he completed an MA in Writing and worked as a communications advisor for one of Australia's largest cemetery trusts. His poems and short stories have appeared in a range of journals, including *Antipodes, Australian Poetry Journal, Cordite, Meanjin, Overland, Rabbit, Short Fiction Journal, Southerly* and *TEXT*.

Alison Whittaker is a Gomeroi poet and academic.

Jessica L Wilkinson has published three poetic biographies, most recently *Music Made Visible: A Biography of George Balanchine* (Vagabond, 2019). She is the founding editor of *Rabbit: a journal for nonfiction poetry* and is a Creative Writing academic at RMIT University.

Panda Wong is a Malaysian-Chinese poet who lives on unceded Wurundjeri land. Her first chapbook *angel wings dumpster fire* was published by Puncher & Wattmann in 2022. Her first EP *salmon cannon me into the abyss*, a collaboration with multiple friends, was released in July 2022.

Jena Woodhouse is the author/translator/compiler of eleven books and chapbooks, six of which are poetry titles. Her latest poetry collection, pending publication, is *Walk like a Wolf*. Her writing has received awards for children's fiction, adult fiction and poetry, and she has been awarded creative residencies and retreats at Hawthornden Castle (Scotland), Camac Centre d'Art (France), The Australian Archaeological Institute at Athens (Greece), The British School at Knossos (Crete) and the Tyrone Guthrie Centre (Ireland).

Grace Yee lives in Melbourne. Her poetry, widely published and anthologised across Australia and overseas, has been awarded the Patricia Hackett Prize, the Peter Steele Poetry Award, and a Creative Fellowship at the State Library Victoria. Grace's debut collection, *Chinese Fish*, is forthcoming with Giramondo Publishing in 2023.

Sista Zai Zanda (Sista Zai/Achihera) has facilitated storytelling workshops in Australia, South Africa, Zimbabwe and Denmark, hosted an opening and closing night at Melbourne Writers Festival, completed the first draft of a work in progress as a recipient of the Neilma Sydney Literary Travel Fund grant and is currently researching for a PhD about Afrofuturism which is supported by the University of Melbourne through a Melbourne Strategic Scholarship. Achihera is a descendant of the Karanga from southeast Zimbabwe and was born and raised in Harare.

Guest Editor Biographies

Jeanine Leane is a Wiradjuri writer, teacher and academic from southwest New South Wales. After a long teaching career, she completed a doctorate in Australian literature and Aboriginal representation and a postdoctoral fellowship at the Australian Centre for Indigenous History at the Australian National University. Her first Volume of poetry, *Dark Secrets After Dreaming: A.D. 1887-1961* (2010, Presspress) won the Scanlon Prize for Indigenous Poetry, 2020 and her first collection of stories, *Purple Press*, won the David Unaipon Award for an unpublished Indigenous writer in 2010. Jeanine has published widely in the area of Aboriginal literature.

*

Judith Beveridge has published seven volumes of poetry all of which have won or been short-listed for major prizes. Her latest volume, *Sun Music: New and Selected Poems* (Giramondo, 2018), won the Prime Minister's Poetry Prize in 2019. She has edited and co-edited a number of anthologies including *Contemporary Australian Poetry*, (Puncher & Wattmann 2016). She was poetry editor for the literary magazine *Meanjin* from 2005-2016. Her work has been studied in schools and universities and translated into many languages. She taught poetry writing at post-graduate level for many years at the University of Sydney and continues to work in the community. She is a recipient of the Philip Hodgins Memorial Medal and the Christopher Brennan Award for excellence in literature.

Acknowledgements and Publication Details

These Acknowledgements include publication or performance Acknowledgements which occurred during the *BoAP 2022* timeframe. We also note if a poem was selected from the open call-out, where it had not been formally published or performed, but had been written and submitted in the timeframe.

Adam Aitken's 'The Far East' appeared in his collection *Revenants*, Giramondo, 2022.

Claire Albrecht's 'I have become psychologically linked to a humpback whale' appeared in her collection *Handshake*, Puncher & Wattmann, March 2022.

Eunice Andrada's 'The Yield' appeared in *Australian Book Review* no. 433, July 2021.

Timmah Ball's 'Songs you can't hear' appeared in *Rabbit* 35, 2022.

Stuart Barnes' 'Sestina: Pain' was shortlisted for the 2021 ACU Prize for Poetry and was published in *ACU Prize for Poetry Anthology* 2021.

Alison J Barton's 'buried light' was selected from the *Best of Australian Poems 2022* open callout. It was subsequently shortlisted for the 2022 Oodgeroo Noonuccal Indigenous Poetry Prize.

Kim Cheng Boey's 'Garden Dreaming' appeared in his collection *The Singer and Others Poems*, Cordite Books, February 2022.

Ken Bolton's 'FOR GIORGIO' was selected from the *Best of Australian Poems 2022* open callout and at this time was unpublished. 'FOR GIORGIO' was later published in Shearsman 133, October 2022.

Peter Boyle's 'After Franz Marc, The Dreamer (1912)' was selected from the *Best of Australian Poems 2022* open callout.

David Brooks' 'Requiem (fire)' appeared in *Meanjin* 81, June 2022.

Jarad Bruinstroop's 'Two Cities' appeared in *HEAT* Series 3 Number 4, Giramondo Publishing, June 2022.

joanne burns' 'peptalk' was selected from *Best of Australian Poems 2022* open callout.

Michelle Cahill's 'Surfacing' was selected from *Best of Australian Poems 2022* open callout.

Bonny Cassidy's 'Mandala' appeared in *Rabbit + Heide, House of Ideas: Modern Women — 12 poets respond to the Heide Museum of Modern Art Exhibition 2021*.

Derek Chan's 'Notes on the After' appeared in *Cordite Poetry Review*, June 2022.

Nandi Chinna's 'The Last Male White Rhinoceros' appeared in *Rabbit* 34, 2021.

Eileen Chong's 'Poem for my Ancestors' was commended in the *Newcastle Poetry Prize 2021* and published in the prize anthology, *Any Saturday, 2021, Running Westward*, October 2021.

Emilie Collyer's 'Photograph: Sunday with Joy Carrying Sweeney at Heide' appeared in *Rabbit + Heide, House of Ideas: Modern Women —12 poets respond to the Heide Museum of Modern Art Exhibition 2021*.

Angela Costi's 'The Heart of the Advocate' appeared in *Westerly* 66.2, November 2021.

Louise Crisp's 'Leafless–Leafs' appeared in *Overland* 244, 2021.

Judith Crispin's 'Purgatory' appeared in *Divining Dante*, Recent Work Press, September 2021.

Sarah Day's 'Penstock Lagoon' appeared in *Overland* 246, Autumn 2022.

Tricia Dearborn's 'Family mathematics' appeared in *Cordite Poetry Review*, August 2021.

Cath Drake's 'Blame the Greenies' was selected from the *Best of Australian Poems 2022* open callout.

Jonathan Dunk's 'natural history poem' appeared in *Going Down Swinging*, September 2021.

Theodore Ell's 'Tenebrae' appeared in *Australian Book Review* no. 442, May 2022 and in his collection *Beginning in Sight*, Recent Work Press, July 2022.

Anne Elvey's 'Coast Banksia' appeared in *The Mind of Plants*, Synergetic Press, October 2021.

Brook Emery's 'Rendezvous' appeared in his collection *Sea Scale: New & Selected Poems*, Puncher & Wattmann, March 2022.

Michael Farrell's '"Australianesque"' appeared in *Australian Book Review* no. 439, January–February 2022 and was shortlisted for the 2022 Peter Porter Poetry Prize.

Dakota Feirer's 'Death by Vertigo' appeared in *Rabbit* 33, 2021.

Luke Fischer's 'Orphic Elegy V' appeared in his collection *A Gamble for my Daughter*, Vagabond Press, March 2022.

Toby Fitch's 'Entanglement' appeared in his collection *Sydney Spleen*, Giramondo Publishing, July 2021 and Red Room Poetry fellowship, August 2021.

Lionel Fogarty's 'All Markets are all Universes' appeared in his collection *Harvest Lingo*, Giramondo Publishing, June 2022.

Es Foong's 'Scar Tissue' appeared in *Rabbit* 33, 2021.

Gavin Yuan Gao's '"COVID"' appeared in *Everything All At Once*, Ultimo Press, November 2021.

Lou Garcia-Dolnik's 'Transported' appeared in *Rabbit + Heide, House of Ideas: Modern Women — 12 poets respond to the Heide Museum of Modern Art Exhibition 2021*.

Chelinay Gates's 'Ruby' appeared in *Westerly* 66.2, November 2021. It was written at the abandoned Bungarun Leprosarium in Derby WA, on an Australia Council for the Arts - Resilience Grant 2020 'Finding Debbie'.

Stephen Gilfedder's 'Canticle for a Dancing Man' appeared in *Westerly* 66.2, November 2021.

Elena Gomez's 'Gunny Sack Rebellion' appeared in *Australian Poetry Journal* 11.2, Australian Poetry, March 2022.

Rory Green's 'Last swim before space flight' appeared in *Meanjin* 80.4, December 2021.

Jennifer Harrison's 'Mandelbrot Set' was selected from the *Best of Australian Poems 2022* open callout. It had been longlisted for the 2022 Peter Porter Poetry Prize and then also appeared in *Australian Book Review* no. 445, August 2022 (published late July).

Dimitra Harvey's 'Cicadas' won the 2021 Queensland Poetry Val Vallis Award and appeared in *Cordite Poetry Review*, October 2021.

Kirwan Henry's 'Last appointment of the day' appeared in *Westerly* 66.2, November 2021.

Barry Hill's 'On Not Cutting Through' appeared in *The Australian*, April 2022.

Maya Hodge's 'quandongs' appeared in *Unyoked Anthology,* November 2021.

Sarah Holland-Batt's 'Pikes Peak' was published in *HEAT* Series 3 Number 1, Giramondo Publishing, June 2022.

Hasib Hourani's 'sealed tight for safety' appeared in *Tell Me Like You Mean It* v5, an Australian Poetry and *Cordite Poetry Review* co-publication, October 2021.

Andy Jackson's 'Ableism is the pre-existing condition that puts us at risk' was selected from the *Best of Australian Poems 2022* open callout. It had also appeared on the Queensland Poetry website in April, 2022.

A Frances Johnson's 'I want/don't want a place' appeared in her collection *Save As*, Puncher & Wattmann, September 2021.

Jill Jones' 'Salt Water Kin' appeared in *Water Lore: Practice, Place and Poetics*, Routledge, May 2022.

Lesh Karan's 'Self-addressed' appeared in *Rabbit* 33, 2021.

Simone King's 'Surfing Again' was published as winner of the 67th Blake Poetry Prize on the website www.westwords.com.au. It was also recited on ABC RN during an interview on the prize in April, 2022.

John Kinsella's 'Rezoning' was selected from the *Best of Australian Poems 2022* open call out. It appeared on *Overland* Friday Features, March 2022.

Yeena Kirkbright's 'Rivers' appeared in *Cordite Poetry Review*, February 2022.

Andy Kissane's 'First Reading' appeared in *Cordite Poetry Review*, August 2021.

Louis Klee's 'Anyhow Poem' appeared in *Australian Poetry Journal* 11.2, Australian Poetry, March 2022.

Kristen Lang's 'Briefly on the Mountain' appeared in *Island* 163, November 2021.

Martin Langford's 'Sea Cliff' was selected from the *Best of Australian Poems 2022* open callout.

Debbie Lim's 'Hummingbird Country' was selected from the *Best of Australian Poems 2022* open callout. It had been shortlisted for the 2022 Peter Porter Poetry Prize and published in *Australian Book Review* no. 439, January–February 2022.

Caitlin Maling's 'Crowning' was selected from the *Best of Australian Poems 2022* open callout.

Jennifer Kemarre Martiniello OAM's 'Being My Grandmothers (after Uluru)' appeared in *Borderless: A transnational anthology of feminist poetry*, Recent Work Press, July 2021.

Glenn McPherson's 'Rain' appeared in *Meanjin* 81.2, June 2022.

Suzi Mezei's 'Extracts' appeared in *Cordite Poetry Review*, February 2022.

Scott-Patrick Mitchell's 'prayer for the parents of every addict' appeared in their collection *Clean*, Upswell Publishing, March 2022.

Audrey Molloy's 'The Earwig' appeared in *Any Saturday*, 2021, *Running Westward*, Newcastle Poetry Prize Anthology, October 2021.

Jazz Money's 'still the night parrot sings' was selected from the *Best of Australian Poems 2022* open callout. It had been written as a response to 'Icarus, my Son', an exhibition by Dean Cross, Goulburn Regional Art Gallery, November 2021–January 2022.

Nicole Jia Moore's 'Migration' appeared in *Rabbit* 33, 2021.

Marjan Mossammaparast's 'Landscapes, with Poem' was selected from the *Best of Australian Poems 2022* callout and had been commissioned for *Cordite: Liminal, Cordite Poetry Review*, May 2022.

Omar Musa's 'Flannel Flowers' appeared in his collection *Killernova*, Penguin, November 2021. It is published here in an updated version by the poet.

Damen O'Brien's 'Your Bones of Glass' was selected from the *Best of Australian Poems 2022* callout.

Thuy On's 'Art for art's sake' appeared in her collection *Decadence*, UWA Publishing, July 2022.

Reneé Pettit-Schipp's 'Elephant Rocks' appeared in *Westerly* 66.2, November 2021.

Felicity Plunkett's 'Talara'tingi' was selected from the *Best of Australian Poems 2022* open callout. The poem was commissioned for the project *Tales From the Herbarium by Plumwood Mountain* and Dr Prudence Gibson.

Claire Potter's 'The Bees' appeared in her collection *Acanthus*, Giramondo Publishing, March 2022.

Kristian Radford's 'Watching Adrienne Lenker Play Guitar with a Paintbrush' appeared in *Cordite Poetry Review*, June 2022.

Harry Reid's 'book of hours' appeared in their collection *Leave Me Alone*, Cordite Books, 1st August 2022.

Nadia Rhook's 'something specific about this boodja' appeared in *Westerly* 66.2, November 2021.

Samah Sabawi's 'Case #70' appeared in *Borderless: A transnational anthology of feminist poetry*, Recent Work Press, July 2021.

Sara M Saleh's 'Live from Gaza' was published in *Rabbit* 34, 2022.

Asiel Adán Sánchez's '43' appeared in *Rabbit*, 34, 2022.

Mykaela Saunders' 'Choice Cuts' appeared in *Overland*, December 2021. It had won the 2020 Oodgeroo Noonuccal Indigenous Poetry Prize.

Brenda Saunders' 'Scarred Landscape' appeared in her collection *Inland Sea*, Ginninderra Press, November 2021.

Leni Shilton's 'Losing Alexandria' was selected from the *Best of Australian Poems 2022* open callout.

Alex Skovron's 'Aubade, Allegro' appeared in his collection *Letters from the Periphery*, Puncher & Wattmann, October 2021.

Yasmin Smith's 'The Saltpan' appeared in *Overland* 243, Winter 2021 (published within timeframe).

David Stavanger's 'recline' appeared in *Cordite Poetry Review*, June 2022.

Josie Jocelyn Suzanne's 'Free Sonnet' appeared in *Westerly* 66.2, November 2021. Translation from the French, original by Renée Vivienne, from her collection *Etudes et Préludes*, Lemarre Publishing, 1909, republished by ErosOnyx 2007, via the University of Michigan.

Isi Unikowski's 'Pumping Station' appeared in *Westerly* 66.2, November 2021.

Ellen van Neerven's 'poem for protection' was performed at 'coven', Emerging Writers' Festival, June 2022.

Saba Vasefi's 'The Portable Home' appeared in Red Room Poetry, June 2022. It had been commissioned by Red Room Poetry as an ekphrastic response to the Art Gallery of NSW's *Shadow Catchers* exhibition, in partnership with Sydney Writers' Festival.

Ann Vickery's 'Buzz Words' appeared in her collection *Bees Do Bother: An Antagonist's Carepack*, Vagabond Press, July 2021.

Anne Walsh's 'The Wolves of Mayo' appeared in *Borderless: A transnational anthology of feminist poetry*, Recent Work Press, July 2021.

Samuel Wagan Watson's 'Closet Monster' appeared in *Meanjin* 81.2, June 2022.

Mitchell Welch's 'Marshmallow flowers' appeared in *Overland* 244, Spring 2021.

Alison Whittaker's 'optimal' appeared in *Borderless: A transnational anthology of feminist poetry*, Recent Work Press, July 2021. It is published here in a version updated by the poet.

Jessica L Wilkinson's 'Art That Moves' was selected from the *Best of Australian Poems 2022* open callout. It was subsequently to be published as a Red Room Poetry 2022 shortlist commission.

Panda Wong's 'signs from the dead' was selected from the *Best of Australian Poems 2022* open callout. It appeared in s*almon cannon me into the abyss* EP, July 2022.

Jena Woodhouse's 'The Weight of Words' was shortlisted for the 2021 ACU Prize and published in 2021 *ACU Prize Anthology*, September 2021.

Grace Yee's 'Tabulations (A Nine Year)' appeared in *Island* 163, October 2021.

Sista Zai Zanda's 'A Poem in Honour of a Lioness Perfecting Her Balance of Inner/Outer Power' appeared in *Borderless: A transnational anthology of feminist poetry*, Recent Work Press, July 2021.